FRANCE 1870-19

D0226242

France 1870–1914

Second Edition

ROBERT GILDEA

LONGMAN
LONDON AND NEW YORK

Addison Wesley Longman Limited
Edinburgh Gate,
Harlow, Essex CM20 2JE,
United Kingdom
and Associated Companies throughout the world

*Published in the United States of America
by Addison Wesley Longman Inc., New York*

First published 1988
Second Edition 1996

ISBN 0 582 292212

British Library Cataloguing in Pubication Data

A catalogue record for this book is available from the British Library

Library of Congress Cataloging-in-Publication Data

Gildea, Robert.
  France, 1870–1914 / Robert Gildea. --2nd ed.
    p. cm. -- (Seminar studies in history)
  Includes bibliographical references and index.
  ISBN 0-582-29221-2
    1. France --History--Third Republic, 1870–1940. 2. France-
  -Politics and government--1870–1914. I. Title. II. Series.
  DC335.G55 1996
  944.081--dc20   96-28653
                                                          CIP

Set by 7 in 10/12 Sabon
Produced through Longman Malaysia, GPS

CONTENTS

Editorial foreword   vii
Note on referencing system   vii
Acknowledgements   viii

PART ONE: THE BACKGROUND   1

1. WHICH REPUBLIC?   1
    The Republic without republicans   5
    The Republic of the republicans   8

PART TWO: ANALYSIS   10

2. THE REPUBLIC OF THE NOTABLES   10
    The President   10
    Ministries   11
    The Senate   11
    The Chamber of Deputies   12
    The commune   14

3. THE CONSTITUTION IN QUESTION   16
    The enemies of Opportunism   17
    Opportunism between Left and Right   19
    Revenge of the disinherited: Boulangism   21

4. SOCIAL STRUCTURE   24
    The peasantry   24
    Workers   26
    The *petite bourgeoisie*   28
    The élite   30

5. SOCIALISM   33
    Party and class: political action and direct action   34
    Revolution or reform?   36
    Anarchism and anarcho-syndicalism   40

6. A CONSERVATIVE REPUBLIC?   42
   Economic protection   42
   The *Ralliement*   43
   Social reform   45
   The restoration of French greatness   49

7. THE DREYFUS AFFAIR   51
   Anti-Semitism   51
   Intellectuals   53
   Politicians   54
   Nationalism   56
   From *mystique* to *politique*   58

8. RADICALISM   60
   What radicalism?   60
   The *Bloc des Gauches*   63
   Class war   65
   Radicals between Revolution and revolution   66

9. NATIONALISM   71
   Defeat   71
   Rebuilding national confidence   72
   The army   73
   Nationalist movements   75
   Towards the *Union Sacrée*   77

PART THREE: CONCLUSION   80

10. THE THIRD REPUBLIC ASSESSED   80

PART FOUR: DOCUMENTS   86

Bibliography   113
Index   125

EDITORIAL FOREWORD

Such is the pace of historical enquiry in the modern world that there is an ever-widening gap between the specialist article or monograph, incorporating the results of current research, and general surveys, which inevitably become out of date. *Seminar Studies in History* are designed to bridge this gap. The books are written by experts in their field who are not only familiar with the latest research but have often contributed to it. They are frequently revised, in order to take account of new information and interpretations. They provide a selection of documents to illustrate major themes and provoke discussion, and also a guide to further reading. Their aim is to clarify complex issues without over-simplifying them, and to stimulate readers into deepening their knowledge and understanding of major themes and topics.

ROGER LOCKYER

NOTE ON REFERENCING SYSTEM

Readers should note that numbers in square brackets [5] refer them to the corresponding entry in the Bibliography at the end of the book (specific page numbers are given in italics). A number in square brackets preceded by *Doc.* [*Doc.* 5] refers readers to the corresponding item in the Documents section which follows the main text.

ACKNOWLEDGEMENTS

I would like to thank Roger Lockyer and W. H. C. Smith for their inspiration and support, the team at Addison Wesley Longman for their clear-sightedness and patience, and my students who over the years have taught me something about this subject.

We are indebted to Éditions Gallimard for permission to reproduce an extract from *Souvenirs sur l'Affaire* by Léon Blum, © Éditions Gallimard, 1935.

While every effort has been made to trace the owners of copyright material, in a few cases this has proved to be problematic and so we take this opportunity to offer our apologies to any copyright holders whose rights we may have unwittingly infringed.

PART ONE: THE BACKGROUND

1 WHICH REPUBLIC?

The Third Republic happened almost by accident, but it was the most successful of all French republics, lasting from 1870 until 1940. The first two French republics had existed respectively for twelve and four years, each of them terminated when a Bonaparte assumed the imperial crown. The Third Republic was given its chance by the defeat of the Second Empire at the hands of Prussia, and would not have emerged so quickly, if at all, without that defeat. There was nothing 'inevitable' about it; indeed the pattern of French history was for monarchy to be displaced by republic, republic by empire and empire by monarchy. It was something of an oddity in the society of nations: France was the only major power in Europe after 1870 that was a republic. But, unlike the First Republic of 1792–1804, the Third Republic did not have to·fight for survival against a coalition of European monarchies. It lived in peace with its neighbours for two generations until 1914, and emerged victorious from the First World War in 1918, before it succumbed to the forces of the Third Reich in 1940 [1–5].

Although the Third Republic was born of military defeat, it is quite legitimate to speak of a republican tradition in France. Or more accurately of strands of a republican tradition, for not all republicans of 1870–1 were in the same vein. One strand was dictatorial and patriotic. These republicans were convinced of the absolute necessity of continuing the war against Prussia after the defeat of the Second Empire in order to preserve the Republic itself. The second element were liberals who thought that the Republic offered the best opportunity to safeguard parliamentary institutions which had been flouted by the Empire. They wanted to make peace with the Prussians as soon as possible, in order to prevent power from falling into the hands of a third group of republicans. These were the insurrectionaries. They were inspired by the Paris Commune of 1792, which had been thrown up by the *sans-culottes* in the teeth of invasion by Prussia and Austria and aristocratic treachery, and which had saved France and founded the First Republic. In similar circumstances they demanded the same desperate measures. Each group of republicans was epitomized by a single personality: the first by Gambetta, the second by Thiers, the third by Blanqui.

Léon Gambetta was a southerner, the son of an Italian grocer, a lawyer, tribune of the people and fierce opponent of the Second Empire. Under the Empire, for the sake of prudence, he and his associates called themselves 'democrats' or 'radicals' rather than republicans. He was a champion of universal suffrage, as the only possible expression of popular sovereignty. This had been established by the Second Republic in 1848, curtailed in 1850 when royalists gained a majority in the Republic, but restored by Louis-Napoleon when he seized power in 1851. The fact that for twenty years universal suffrage had played into the hands of the Second Empire did not cause Gambetta to change his mind: the people would in time have to be educated in republican principles [6]. For Gambetta was a republican as well as a democrat. He believed that the Republic was the embodiment of the French Revolution, a militant regime that roared defiance at monarchies and empires alike. He hoped that the Republic would be restored legally rather than by revolution, and when republicans increased their representation in the Legislative Body from 35 to 87 seats in 1869, he set about organizing them into a viable force [*Doc. 1a*]. The Second Empire in fact received a new lease of life in May 1870 when a new liberal constitution was massively ratified by plebiscite. Gambetta had to confess that it was stronger than ever. Four months later Napoleon III was defeated at Sedan, and republican deputies proclaimed the Republic in Paris on 4 September.

A Government of National Defence was immediately set up to continue the war against the Prussians. The whole of northern France was occupied, Paris was cut off on 19 September, and in provincial towns such as Lyon and Marseille republican groups seized power and set up regional federations of republican strongholds in order to carry on the struggle as best they could [7]. Gambetta emerged as the key figure in the Government of National Defence. As Minister for War, he was determined to win at any cost. This meant reinforcing the depleted regular army by raising an auxiliary citizen army which would fight alongside it [8]. As Minister of the Interior, he tried to bring the provinces under his direct control by the appointment of republican prefects he could trust. Pressure was growing for the calling of a National Assembly to draw up a new constitution. Gambetta resisted this, fearing that such an assembly would be dominated by Bonapartists and royalists rather than republicans. A republican dictatorship was necessary in his eyes to preserve the Republic itself [9].

Not all the members of the Government of National Defence agreed with Gambetta. Foremost among these was Adolphe Thiers, an opposition journalist under the Restoration and many times minister under the July Monarchy. He was a liberal and parliamentarian, who detested universal suffrage, and had supported the disenfranchisement of three million of the 'vile multitude' in 1850. He believed that universal suffrage was fickle and irrational, played into the hands of demagogues and warmongers, and should be limited to the educated and propertied. Unlike Gambetta, he wanted to conclude an armistice as soon as possible with Prussia, and to hold elections for a National Assembly which would ratify peace terms. Thiers had his way. An armistice was signed in January 1871, and the following month elections were held. The electorate's priorities were peace and liberty. At the polls it rejected Bonapartists and Gambettist republicans as (in different ways) warmongering and dictatorial, and returned a stream of royalists, including two Orleanist princes. While criticizing universal suffrage, Thiers himself was fairly indifferent as to which regime was best for France. In 1850 he had argued that conservatives were divided between three dynasties and the Republic and that therefore a republic was the regime that divided them least. In 1870 he was delighted to see the end of the Second Empire but now that a republic had been declared he wanted no truck with dangerous plans to restore the monarchy. As he had been elected in twenty-seven departments (elections were on a system of departmental proportional representation and candidates could stand in more than one department) he was the obvious choice to be entrusted with executive power by the National Assembly. He was elected Chief of the Executive Power of the French Republic on 13 February 1871 and sought to keep on board both republicans for the business of making a difficult peace, and royalists in order to negotiate a conservative, parliamentary regime. The government he appointed included one confirmed royalist, three confirmed republicans and five, including himself, uncommitted. The final decision about the regime was yet to be taken [10].

Paris, meanwhile, which had been under Prussian siege since September 1870, was seething with revolutionaries who had no confidence either in the Government of National Defence or in the

National Assembly. First, there were Blanquists – comrades of Auguste Blanqui, an exponent of armed insurrection since 1830 and himself currently in prison [11]. Next, there were the Jacobins around Charles Delescluze who, unlike Gambetta, was a veteran of 1848 and was prepared to use revolutionary means in order to obtain a government fully accountable to the people. Finally, there were the adherents of the First Workers' International, grouped in sections and trade unions, numbering between 20,000 and 30,000 workers. The revolutionaries demanded direct democracy, or the retention of power in the hands of the people, not their elected representatives. The instruments of their power were: first, vigilance committees in each of the twenty *arrondissements* of Paris, to keep often moderate mayors in revolutionary step [*Doc. 1b*]; second, the National Guard, which had been banned under the Empire but was expanded by Gambetta to defend Paris, and had swollen to about 360,000; and third, revolutionary clubs, the foci of heated political debate. The goal of the revolutionaries was the establishment of a central revolutionary organ to save Paris and the Republic. The enemy were both the Prussians who paraded insolently on the Champs Elysées in Paris by permission of Thiers on 1 March and those Frenchmen who believed that social order was more important than victory, and that the peace agreed by the National Assembly would have to be imposed on Paris by disarming the National Guard [12].

On 18 March 1871 regular troops were sent into Paris to seize the cannon held by the National Guard. But they were too few and unreliable, and many fraternized with the National Guard and the working-class populations of the suburbs who rose in their support. The central committee of the National Guard battalions, formed on 15 March, became a provisional revolutionary government in Paris as the executive power withdrew in disarray to Versailles. On 26 March a Commune to represent the whole of Paris (for the first time since the 1790s) was elected. It was dominated by National Guard militants, Blanquists, Jacobins, Internationalists and other socialists. For weeks the troops of the Commune and those of the government at Versailles were locked in combat, with the execution of hostages on both sides. But, once the peace with newly-united Germany was signed at Frankfurt, the balance of forces shifted to Thiers, as Bismarck allowed 60,000 French prisoners of war to pass through German lines and attack Paris. In the brutal suppression of the *Semaine Sanglante* (Bloody Week) 25,000 Parisians were massacred. Of the 40,000 arrested, 10,000 were convicted, 5,000 sent to the penal colony of New Caledonia in the Pacific, 93 condemned to death and 23 executed. The Republic of Monsieur Thiers triumphed over the workers' Republic of the Commune, but the memory and mythology of the Commune would continue to define working-class culture and consciousness and perpetuate an irrational fear of class war among French property-owners.

THE REPUBLIC WITHOUT REPUBLICANS

After the Commune a Catholic noble, Albert de Mun, who had been taken prisoner by the Prussians at Metz and then released to help with its suppression, observed that the Republic 'seemed dishonoured for ever' [13 *p. 57*]. A great chance to restore the monarchy presented itself. Many conservatives believed that only the monarchy could guarantee religion, the family and private property. The National Assembly repealed the law of exile which banned heads of the royal families; and the two pretenders – the Comte de Chambord and the Comte de Paris, respectively grandsons of Charles X and Louis-Philippe, Legitimist and Orleanist – returned to France [14].

However, things were not so simple. The reason given by many historians for the failure of restoration at this point is that on 5 July 1871 the Comte de Chambord, who had spent most of his life in exile in Austria, issued a manifesto saying that he would never give up the white flag of Henri IV (which in any case had been regularly used as the royal flag only since 1815) [*Doc. 2a*]. But the explanation cannot be reduced to the foibles of one man. Royalists included politicians as well as pretenders. The problem was that Chambord failed to consult with the grand old man of royalism in France, the Comte de Falloux, who was obliged to deal in the art of the possible. And in 1871 the plain fact was that only 80 deputies on the extreme Right of the National Assembly accepted the manifesto [15]; the so-called moderate Right and the centre Right (or Orleanists) did not. Failure to consult was symptomatic of something else: Chambord wanted the restoration of a 'real' monarchy, which he variously called 'traditional', 'tutelary' or 'tempered'. It was not absolute monarchy, but it was not constitutional monarchy either. Unfortunately the vast majority of royalist deputies wanted a constitutional, parliamentary monarchy which left power in *their* hands. The lessons of 1830 and of the authoritarian Empire had not been learned in vain [*Doc. 2b*].

While the royalists argued among themselves, Gambetta was

stumping the country, delivering speeches and working to recreate the image of the Republic. Above all it had to be dissociated from that of the Commune. Gambetta claimed that the republicans were the party of order; those who opposed the Republic presently established were the sedition-mongers. Republicans did not represent social revolution, he argued, because there was 'no social question', no inevitable condition of class struggle, but rather a widening access to property as a result of hard work, saving and education. Republicans were not the propertyless proletarians who had set Paris alight but the 'new social strata', the tradesmen, small manufacturers and farmers who, he said, had been thrown up by the industrial revolution and universal suffrage and were now eagerly waiting to take power from the old élites that had been cosseted by the monarchy and Empire [16].

The tide began to move in the direction of republicanism. Republicans did well in the by-elections of July 1871. Thiers, who was elected President of the Republic by the National Assembly, declared himself squarely in favour of the Republic at the beginning of the parliamentary session in November 1872. In order to retain a breadth of support on the Right, he declared, 'the Republic will be conservative, or it will not exist' [*Doc. 3*]. His ideal was a presidential Republic, which vested most power in himself. Increasingly, however, the man who had negotiated peace and saved France from the Commune became suspect to the Right. They wanted not a presidential but a parliamentary constitution, under which ministers would be responsible to them. And they did not trust Thiers to be a strong enough bulwark against the rising tide of republicanism. The crunch came in April 1873, when in a by-election which polled the whole of Paris, Thiers's candidate, none other than his foreign minister, was defeated by the candidate of the radical Left, who had been approved by Gambetta. On 24 May 1873, Thiers was overturned by a majority composed of royalists and Bonapartists [17].

With Thiers gone there was again the possibility of a royalist restoration. The new president might have been the Orleanist Duc d'Aumale, but the (Legitimist) extreme Right objected, so the nomination went instead to a military man who had loyally served every regime since the Restoration, Marshal MacMahon. Nothing was settled yet. During the summer of 1873 royalist leaders were deep in conference. The Orleanist pretender, the Comte de Paris, agreed to defer to the claim of the Legitimist branch. The understanding was that he would succeed on the death of the Comte de Chambord, who was childless. But again Chambord slighted royalist notables by refusing to accept the tricolor, which was, after all, the flag not only of the Republic but of the constitutional monarchies of 1791 and 1830 and of the French army. Further, he refused to surrender his title in favour of the Orleanist branch, a gesture which would have saved his honour and France for the monarchy. In the absence of 'fusion', as the reconciliation of the claims of the rival branches was called, a consensus of conservatives was possible only *within* the Republic. On 20 November 1873 the royalist and Bonapartist majority in the National Assembly agreed to extend the presidential powers of MacMahon for seven years.

Chambord and the hard-line Legitimists were not the only obstacle to a royalist restoration. MacMahon took as his prime minister the Orleanist Duc de Broglie, and the Orleanists were anxious to establish a constitution as much like that of 1830 as possible. This would involve a Second Chamber that was largely appointed, and, in elections to the First Chamber, significant restrictions on universal suffrage. But universal suffrage was untouchable in the eyes of both republicans and Bonapartists and to abrogate it would only serve to give them a powerful rallying cry. De Broglie was toppled by an 'unholy' alliance of republicans, Bonapartists and Legitimists in May 1874. The Orleanists were now stranded. Moreover, they had reason to fear a revival of Bonapartism which, having been roundly beaten at the polls in 1871, won a series of by-elections in 1874. The Bonapartists argued that the Empire had been terminated by events; the people had not been consulted on the regime since the plebiscite of May 1870. They proposed the dissolution of the bickering National Assembly and a plebiscite which, they thought, would restore the Emperor's son, the Prince Imperial [18].

The Orleanists had no choice but to reach an understanding with moderate republicans on the establishment of a parliamentary Republic which alone would keep Bonapartists, Legitimists and radicals out of power. It would be based on universal suffrage, but the Orleanists insisted on a Second Chamber as a condition of their support. This conjunction of centres was not extraordinary, but represented a natural coalition of talent, wealth and birth. Key negotiations took place between the Orleanist Duc d'Audiffret Pasquier and Auguste Casimir-Périer, a republican in the manner of Thiers, but the son of one of Louis-Philippe's prime ministers and Pasquier's brother-in-law and neighbour on the Champs Elysées. By February 1875 a constitution had been hammered out. There would be a Chamber of Deputies and a Senate, which together would elect a president of the Republic. The president had the right to dissolve the Chamber, but only with the approval of the Senate. Whereas the July Monarchy was a king surrounded by republican institutions, this was a Republic surrounded by monarchical institutions [4 *p. 40*].

THE REPUBLIC OF THE REPUBLICANS

The constitution was firmly on paper; but it remained to be seen how it would operate in practice. In the first elections to the Chamber under the constitution, in February 1876, the republicans obtained a majority while the Orleanists, together with an alliance of Bonapartists and Legitimists, went down heavily. However, the Senate elected the previous month was in the hands of conservatives and conservative elements also dominated the magistracy, bureaucracy and army. This permitted MacMahon to appoint prime ministers not from the republican majority but from former ministers of Thiers, such as Jules Simon, who described himself as 'profoundly conservative and profoundly republican' [19 *p. 206–7*]. The principle of ministerial responsibility – that the composition of the ministry should reflect the parliamentary majority – was far from being established. This, however, was precisely what Gambetta and the republicans wished to establish. Gambetta indicted Simon's irresoluteness towards the pretensions of the Catholic Church – his famous cry was 'Clericalism, there is the enemy!' – in order to identify Simon with the Catholic Right and disqualify him as a republican. MacMahon, for his part, decided that Simon was not resolute enough against the pretensions of the republicans. On 16 May 1877 he dismissed Simon and replaced him with the Duc de Broglie, who formed a ministry of Orleanists and Bonapartists. The Chamber of Deputies was prorogued for a month and when it reconvened on 16 June it heard that the President had obtained the support of the Senate for the dissolution of the Chamber. This was within the letter of the constitution, but hardly in its spirit. The outraged republicans passed a vote of censure on the ministry by 363 votes to 158 [*Doc. 4*].

Elections were held in October 1877. The government used all the means of pressure refined by the authoritarian Empire in order to break the republican majority. The republicans riposted by attacking the clericalism and Bonapartism of the government. The government failed. It took only 40 seats from the republicans who won an immense moral victory. MacMahon was obliged to admit one of the republican majority, Charles de Freycinet, to the Cabinet. The municipal elections of January 1878 were a 'town-hall revolution' with republicans sweeping to power in thousands of communes. Busts of Marianne, symbol of the Republic, wearing a phrygian bonnet in the name of liberty, were placed in town halls all over France [20] and on 30 June 1878 towns and villages celebrated the inauguration of the republican Republic, hanging out tricolor flags and applauding bands playing the *Marseillaise*. Because senators were indirectly elected by colleges composed for the most part of mayors, the effect of the town hall revolution was felt when the Senate was renewed in January 1879. The republicans acquired a majority there as well. This was decisive. Marshal MacMahon resigned as President and the two chambers elected in his place a died-in-the-wool republican, the 71-year-old Jules Grévy. Gambetta became speaker of the Chamber of Deputies.

The constitution of the Third Republic was established by compromise but compromise was no longer possible. The 16 May was regarded by the republicans as a *coup d'état* against the constitution, scarcely less evil than that of the 2 December 1851. Those who numbered among the 363 were immortalized as the preservers of republican legitimacy and crowned in glory. Those who had supported the *coup* were judged to have disqualified themselves for ever from office in the Republic. From now on, ministries were required to command not just a majority in the Chamber of Deputies but a majority of *republicans*. Politics in the Third Republic was henceforth to revolve around the strict principle of republican legitimacy: only legitimate republicans could claim to rule; the others were condemned to look on in impotence [21].

PART TWO: ANALYSIS

2   THE REPUBLIC OF THE NOTABLES

THE PRESIDENT

The Third Republic was a parliamentary not a presidential Republic
[22]. The president was elected not directly by the people, as in
1848, but indirectly, by deputies and senators sitting together and
assembled for that purpose at Versailles. This was clearly to prevent
the emergence of another Bonaparte. (Direct presidential elections
were not reintroduced until 1962.) By the same token the president
was not responsible to the people, as Napoleon III had been – a
position which conferred immense authority. Neither was he
responsible to parliament, as Thiers had been in 1871. This was the
position of ministers. It was impossible for parliament to force a
president to resign; however a ministerial 'strike' or collective refusal
to serve in a cabinet under him could achieve this by another route.
The president had the right to dissolve the Chamber of Deputies, if
he had the agreement of the Senate, but no president attempted this
after 16 May 1877; the lesson had been learned. Even so, the
powers of the president were not negligible. He had the direction of
foreign policy: the Franco-Russian alliance was very much the
personal triumph of Sadi Carnot. The president chose the president
of the council of ministers (the technical name for the prime
minister): Grévy was able to keep out an extremist like Gambetta
and preferred moderates like Freycinet and Ferry until the shift to
the left in the elections of 1881 forced his hand. Even then,
Gambetta was allowed to do his worst and fell after two months.
The president was also able to exert pressure to influence the
composition of cabinets: Grévy insisted that ministries reflect not
only the parliamentary majority but also the temper of the country
as a whole [23].

MINISTRIES

Parliament was the constitutional centre of gravity in the Third Republic. This was a deliberate rehabilitation following the Second Empire, when it had been firmly subordinated to the executive. Deputies had the right to interpellate ministries – that is, to demand an account of men and measures – and to propose votes of no confidence. This tended to produce a rapid turnover of ministries: there were 108 between 1870 and 1940, averaging eight months each. Such statistics seem to support the thesis of ministerial instability in the Third Republic. But factors promoting stability must also be examined. The fall of a ministry did not entail a general election, only the formation of a new ministry. A 'new' ministry was often only a 'replastering' of the old one, with the introduction of some ministers to reflect the colour of the victorious majority, but many of the old faces were carried over too. In the period of the so-called Opportunist Republic (1879–93), a pool of no more than six or seven ministers formed the basis of almost every ministry. Recognized *ministrables* – those clearly eligible for office – constantly shadowed those actually in office. And while ministries rose and fell, ministers often had very long careers. Thus Freycinet was continuously in office between 1888 and 1893, as was Delcassé between 1898 and 1905 [24].

Ministries were responsible to parliament, and had to command a majority there to survive. The invocation of the principle of republican legitimacy required more specifically that a majority of republican deputies support it. This ruled out the possibility of *alternance* between ministries of the Left and ministries of the Right. Even if there was a dominance of centrist feeling in the country at large, this could not be translated into a conjunction of centres in parliament. The consensus of 1875 had been destroyed by the crisis of 16 May 1877. Ministries which were seen to rely on the votes of the Right, such as that of Rouvier in 1887 or Méline in 1896, were fiercely challenged in the Chamber. The role of the Senate was less clear. After 16 May, when it had approved the presidential *coup*, it was confined to a subordinate position. Yet it was not a negligible factor. It managed to topple the radical ministry of Léon Bourgeois in 1896, even though Bourgeois had a majority in the Chamber.

THE SENATE

The Senate was a present given to the Orleanists in return for their acceptance of universal suffrage. A single chamber brought back memories of the Convention parliament of 1792, forum of the Jacobins and a prey to radical clubs and popular demonstrations, even though single chambers in 1849 and 1871 had been dominated by royalists. The Senate was to provide some insulation of the political system against overheating by universal suffrage. It was elected indirectly by colleges of mayors and councillors of departmental and *arrondissement* assemblies, and described by Gambetta as the 'Grand Council of the Communes of France' [16 *p. 242*]. The countryside and small towns were over-represented in the Senate, while large towns were under-represented, which gave rise to the epithet the 'Chamber of Agriculture'. Senators were elected for nine years (as against four years for deputies), the Senate being renewed by one-third every three years, to ensure continuity. This meant that an outgoing senator might be thirteen or fifteen years on from a direct consultation of the people. The republicans refused to accept the Orleanists' desire for nominated senators, but one-quarter of the Senate were originally elected as life-senators. This system was terminated in 1884, though life-senators in post were allowed to continue for life.

Although it occupied second place to the Chamber, the Senate was not powerless. Its majority after 1879 was republican, but it was above all a centrist majority which disliked extremes. It stood out against anticlerical legislation, progressive income tax and parliamentary reform. Jules Ferry called it the 'fortress of the Republic' [21 *p. 244*], by which he meant that it offered stout resistance to the tyranny of popular opinion, and in particular to public opinion whipped up by demagogues like Boulanger. The Senate provided a secure and honourable retirement for politicians, but in its own right nurtured leaders of the nation. Between 1898 and 1914 it provided eight of the thirteen presidents of the council and three presidents of the Republic: Loubet, Fallières and Poincaré [25].

THE CHAMBER OF DEPUTIES

The Chamber of Deputies was directly elected by universal manhood suffrage. In 1871 this operated under a system of departmental proportional representation, which obliged candidates to present themselves on a list (the so-called *scrutin de liste*). This gave way in 1875 to a system of single-member constituencies, of which there might be four, six or eight to a department. Such constituencies had a tendency to become 'fiefs' of sitting deputies, who were often local men who had come up through the regular channel of mayor and departmental councillor before their election to parliament [26]. Two-thirds of all deputies between 1870 and 1940 held on to their seats for an average period of fourteen years [27]. This system was detested by Gambetta and the radical republicans, who argued that it was too vulnerable to local interests, and that only the restoration of the *scrutin de liste* would create a clear republican majority to back a decisive republican government. Two attempts by Gambetta to restore departmental lists were defeated in 1881 and 1882 before they were tried again in 1885, but this had the effect of increasing the representation of radicals and conservatives at the expense of moderate republicans, and then of allowing Boulangism to gain a hold. The single-member constituencies were restored in 1889.

Under the Second Empire (and in 1877) the Ministry of the Interior and the prefects – the government's agents in each department – tended to promote 'official candidates' who were well-disposed to the government and managed the elections for them. Under the Third Republic, influence shifted towards the deputies [28]. Ministries needed their support in votes of confidence, and had to deal with them individually, because there were no organized parties. Deputies were prepared to give that support in exchange for favours for their constituents, to help the process of re-election. Such favours included scholarships at the local *lycée*, exemption from compulsory military service, jobs ranging from a prefectship to running a tobacconist's shop (tobacco was a government monopoly), the suspension of judicial proceedings against cafés for infringing the licensing laws (cafés were often centres of political meeting and support), and contracts and concessions for railway companies and other businesses. The government was not wholly without influence. 'Ministerial' deputies obtained favours; those opposed to the ministry did not, and had to use other means to secure constituents' votes, such as the threat of eviction from farms or harnessing the support of the clergy. It was not unknown for the children of those who voted against the local landowner to be prohibited from taking their first communion.

The republican notables of 1880 were most unlike the republican militants who were punished after Louis-Napoleon's *coup d'état* in 1851. In the southern department of the Gard the vast majority of the militants had been peasants, artisans and intellectuals, while 74 per cent of the notables were landowners, merchants, industrialists, professional men or civil servants. As the Republic became established, so republicanism became more bourgeois. The profile of deputies in 1877 and 1885 confirms this picture: 89 per cent came from the same landed, business, professional and official categories. Similar social backgrounds often meant that friendships were formed across political barriers. The Palais Bourbon was something of a club. As Robert de Jouvenel said in 1914, 'There is less difference between two deputies, one of whom is a revolutionary and the other not, than between two revolutionaries, one of whom is a deputy and the other not' [29 *p. 17*].

Despite the distinctly bourgeois nature of deputies, they were not in a very easy position financially. The salary was a meagre 9,000 francs after 1871 – less than they had been paid under the Second Empire and equivalent to the salary of a tax inspector, a colonel in the artillery or a headmaster of a Paris *lycée* (a senior prefect might earn 35,000 francs in 1880). Deputies' salaries rose to 15,000 francs only in 1907, when ministers were paid a handsome 60,000 francs. The other side of their independence from party discipline was the lack of expenses from any party to fight elections. And the cost of elections, of course, was very high. Control of a local newspaper to put across their views was essential for deputies. Most canvassing took place in cafés and the candidate was expected to be generous. At election time it helped to give charity to hospitals, compensate communes for flood-damage or buy new uniforms for the firemen. Here is the root of what has often been dismissed as the corruption and venality of Third Republic politicians [30] [*Doc. 5*]. Given the huge bills they had to meet, it was attractive to them to be offered funds or directorships by financial, industrial or colonial enterprises which were themselves seeking contracts and concessions from the government. Business, the press and politics interlocked very closely under the Third Republic.

THE COMMUNE

The 36,000 communes were the cells of French political life. Each commune had it's mayor and municipal council, with the exception of Paris, which had a municipal council but no mayor. In the municipal elections of 1878 and 1881 the republicans came to power in thousands of communes, and in 1882 municipal councillors were given the right to elect the mayor from their own number, rather than having him chosen by the administration. The replacement of old élites by new social strata in local government has been demonstrated by a study of the wine-growing districts of Mâcon and Chalon-sur-Saône in Burgundy [31]. In 1878 notables (landowners, merchants and liberal professions) were still dominant, but by 1912 they accounted for only one-quarter of mayors. In this period, power in the countryside shifted from landowners living off rents to medium proprietors farming their own land. It is often argued that rural populations were ignorant of, or indifferent to, national issues. This was not the case. In the first place, mayors, whether of large urban communes or small rural ones, were involved in national celebrations along the lines of the Fête de la Fédération of 1790. A banquet organized by the Paris municipal council and presided over by the president of the Republic to mark the centenary of the French Revolution in 1889 was attended by 11,000 mayors, and a similar banquet in 1900 in the context of the Universal Exposition was attended by 20,000 mayors. Secondly, the burning question of the 1880s was whether religious congregations or lay teachers should teach in the schools maintained by communes, while that of the 1900s was whether the congregations, expelled from the communal schools, should be allowed to run their own private schools. These controversies linked every commune in France to political battles going on in parliament, and ensured that the axis of French politics, which divided anticlerical from clerical, republican from conservative, blue from white (to use the terms forged during the French Revolution), ran through every region of France, dividing commune from commune and sometimes, within the commune, family from family [32]. The irony was that the school question, by polarising politics along religious lines, and clienteles respectively behind conservative and republican notables (thus hindering the emergence of social issues and the polarization of politics along class lines), actually promoted stability in the Third Republic.

3 THE CONSTITUTION IN QUESTION

For the first thirty years of the Republic the question of the legitimacy of the Republic underscored the essential difference between Left and Right. The school question, dividing anticlerical from clerical, was really a battle for the survival of the Republic. The question of the working class was subordinated to this higher cause: their grievances could not be attended to so long as the existence of the regime was in doubt. Similarly, the nascent movement to claim equal rights of citizenship for women could find no space to express itself. Indeed, because women's organizations were persecuted alongside radical and socialist ones by the conservative governments of the mid-1870s, women's leaders tended of their own accord to put the defence of the anticlerical Republic first [33].

However, neither Right nor Left was monolithic. On the republican side there were men of 1848 who had been persecuted after 1851, veterans of the Paris Commune (many in exile of a forced or voluntary nature before 1880), patriots of 1870, and those who had rallied late in the day from Bonapartism or Orleanism. In the 1880s they tended to fall into two main camps, the moderates or Opportunists, and the radicals. On many issues they divided, but in the last resort, when the republican principle itself was threatened, they pulled together under the slogan of 'republican concentration'. The Right was fragmented in its own way. One problem was dynastic, in that there were three rival monarchical claims: Legitimist, Orleanist and Bonapartist. More subtly, there were differences between those who were irreducibly opposed to the Republic as such, and those who were prepared to compromise with the regime, so long as they were given a chance to enter a governing majority, influence policy and one day themselves hold office. Unfortunately the principle of republican legitimacy ruled this out of order. The Right was condemned to exclusion on what seemed to be a permanent basis. The pattern of politics which now became a risk was the following: that the moderate republicans or Opportunists would find themselves isolated from the radicals, and though inclined for practical reasons to seek accommodation with the moderate Right, they might be prohibited by their own principles from doing so. A corollary of this was that an alliance of some sort might be formed between radicals and the Right, for they had at least one thing in common: a desire to get the Opportunists out of power. This alliance in the late 1880s took the form of Boulangism.

THE ENEMIES OF OPPORTUNISM

The rivalry between Opportunists and radicals in the republican movement was epitomized by the rivalry between Jules Ferry and Georges Clemenceau. Both had been fierce opponents of the Second Empire, but Ferry was a rich bourgeois who married into the wealthy Scheurer-Kestner family, while Clemenceau, rejected by the same family, went to seek his fortune in the United States and had a disastrous marriage with an American. Ferry was mayor of Paris during the siege of 1870 and was driven from the Hôtel de Ville by the Paris Commune; ever afterwards he nurtured a hatred of the Paris mob, which was mutual, and stood for a rural constituency in the Vosges. Clemenceau, by contrast, as mayor of the Montmartre *arrondissement* of Paris in 1870–1, tried to mediate between the insurgents and the government, cultivated working-class support without being a socialist, and was a deputy for Paris between 1876 and 1885 [34, 35].

Radicals and Opportunist disagreed on a number of fundamental issues. The radicals were keen to amnesty the Communards but the Opportunists refused to do this until 'the opportune time', which turned out to be in June 1880 [36]. The radicals were passionate anticlericals who demanded the expulsion of religious congregations from state schools and the abolition of the Concordat of 1801 by which the state funded the Catholic Church in return for control over it. Gambetta, technically an Opportunist but a thorn in Ferry's side, adopted the rhetoric of militant anticlericalism to please them, especially when he toured the Midi [*Doc. 6a*]. Jules Ferry, as Minister of Education, expelled the Jesuits from élite colleges in 1879 and established free, compulsory, lay primary education, banning the catechism and clergy from state schools, under laws of 1881 and 1882. He instituted moral and civic education instead, to forge a body of citizens who would support the Republic. But he also saw that to persecute the Catholic Church would undermine the Republic, and thus he was happy to leave individual communes to decide whether they wished to expel religious congregations from state schools and was keen to preserve the Concordat. [*Doc. 6b*].

The most important apple of discord was the constitution of 1875. Radicals regarded it as a fudge, cobbled together to please the Orleanists. They wanted a constitution genuinely responsive to the people, on the model of the Convention parliament of 1792–5. They accepted the presidency once it became republican in 1879, but demanded the abolition of the Senate and the restoration of departmental lists for the election of deputies. Ferry, who was prime minister in 1880–1 and 1883–5, wanted a parliamentary constitution insulated against popular power and a strong government no longer at the mercy of shifting parliamentary majorities. He defended the Senate and the right – discredited after 1877 – of the president with the consent of the Senate to dissolve a hostile Chamber. In the event, departmental lists were conceded for 1885 and life-senators were abolished, but the Senate itself survived.

Radicals differed from Opportunists also in the priority they gave to social reform. They pressed for the nationalization of the railway companies, whereas the Opportunist government preferred to expand the railway network in conjunction with the 'big six' railway companies, funding them and guaranteeing the loans they raised [37]. The radicals wanted free trade, in order to provide cheap food for workers; the Opportunists agreed to 'Corn Laws' in 1885 for the benefit of landowners [38]. Radicals demanded rights for trade unions, which were indeed conceded in 1884, but with the aim, in the government's eyes, of separating organized labour from socialist agitators. The last bone of contention was foreign policy. Establishing colonies in North Africa and Indo-China was the Opportunists' way of redeeming national honour without antagonizing Bismarck. Radicals were unimpressed. They argued that colonies served the interests of banks, railway companies, the steel industry and arms manufacturers, while ordinary Frenchmen had to pay the taxes and fight the battles. More than that, they adopted a patriotic stance, pointing out that Germany was the real enemy, and must be faced in the Vosges, not in Vietnam [39]. Outside parliament a *Ligue des Patriotes* was set up by Paul Déroulède in 1882 to mobilise veterans, educate youth in the patriotic spirit, press for *revanche* (revenge) against Germany and generally embarrass the Opportunist oligarchy [40]. Inside parliament Georges Clemenceau managed to bring down Opportunist ministries on three colonial entanglements, in Tunisia,

Egypt and Indo-China. The danger to Opportunist governments was especially great when radicals were able to call on the support of royalists and Bonapartists. The colonial, anticlerical and economic policies of the government helped to revive the fortunes of the Right, and in turn the strategies of the Right became more sophisticated [41]. In 1878, Albert de Mun had dared to salute an 'imminent counter-revolution' but was firmly slapped down by the Legitimist leader, the Comte de Falloux [42]. Softly, softly, was the order of the day. The intransigent Comte de Chambord died in 1883, leaving the Orleanist Comte de Paris as sole royalist pretender, and a royalist parliamentarian, the Baron de Mackau, set up a Union of the Right which used the term 'conservative' rather than 'royalist' in order to blur its opposition to the regime and widen its base. Napoleon III's son, the Prince Imperial, died fighting the Zulus in South Africa in 1879 and the new pretender, Prince Jérôme-Napoleon (cousin of the late Emperor and nicknamed Plon-Plon) published a manifesto in 1883 which floated the idea of a revision of the constitution in favour of direct presidential elections. This was intended to appeal to radicals disenchanted with the Opportunist Republic. but it alienated conservative Bonapartists led by Paul de Cassagnac, who preferred an Orleanist monarchy to a Bonapartism which no longer dreamed of restoring the Empire, and allied with the Union of the Right.

OPPORTUNISM BETWEEN LEFT AND RIGHT

In the elections of October 1885 the Right made a strong comeback, and the Opportunists were driven belatedly into an alliance of 'republican concentration' with the Radicals in order to keep the Right out of power. The Opportunists numbered 201 in the new Chamber against 180 radicals and far Left and 203 conservatives (including about 100 royalists and 50 Bonapartists). They had survived only by courtesy of the radicals and for the first time had to concede ministerial posts to them. President Grévy refused to take the radical Floquet as prime minister, but appointed Freycinet and then (December 1886) the radical René Goblet. General Georges Boulanger, a school friend and protégé of Clemenceau, became Minister of War. The radicals forced through their own policies. Religious congregations were expelled from state primary schools. After the marriage of the daughter of the Comte de Paris to the Crown Prince of Portugal in Paris in May 1886, which looked like a gathering of the Orleanist court, a law was passed exiling the heads and heirs of previous reigning families. Boulanger started to republicanize the army, where the officer corps was still very royalist and imperialist. Four Orleanist princes were relieved of their commands, royalist garrisons were shifted into republican towns, and a new military law (eventually passed in 1889) imposed three years' service on all young men, ending exemption for seminarists and the wealthy.

Boulanger's special turn was to threaten *revanche* against Germany, to the delight of his revolutionary-patriotic supporters. However, Bismarck took his threats seriously, called up the reserve and (after new elections) had the Reichstag agree to enlarge the German army. This frightened Jules Ferry and the Opportunists, who, to avert the danger of war, allied with the Right to overthrow the radical-infested Goblet ministry and Boulanger with it. Ferry now started to look at the possibility of discarding the straitjacket of a republican legitimacy and of bringing conservatives into an Opportunist-led ministry without the radicals, whom he now considered a threat to peace and parliamentary government. Some conservatives were thinking along similar lines. The Bonapartist deputy Edgar Raoul-Duval, had launched a paper in November 1886 (shortly after the Whigs had defected to the Tories in Great Britain in opposition to Irish Home Rule) in which he asked, 'Why can't we have *our* Whigs and Tories?' [43 *p. 615*]. President Grévy consulted Baron de Mackau of the Union of the Right, and secured the support of sufficient numbers of conservatives for an Opportunist ministry under the banker Maurice Rouvier, without radicals and without Boulanger. Boulanger was sent off to take command of an army corps well out of the way in Clermont-Ferrand. The situation, however, was far from stabilized. Boulanger's departure from the Gare de Lyon in July 1887 was the occasion of a huge demonstration orchestrated by Déroulède and the *Ligue des Patriotes*. The radicals decided to bring down Grévy, who had been re-elected for a second term in 1885, by exposing a scandal. Grévy's son-in-law, Daniel Wilson, was accused of managing an agency in the Elysée Palace which sold recommendations for honours, and was arrested. Since the President was not formally responsible, the radicals secured the help of the Right to topple Rouvier (November 1887) and then organized a boycott of ministers. Freycinet, Goblet and Clemenceau (even he was asked) declined to form a cabinet. Grévy was obliged to resign [44].

The task in December 1887 was to find a new president. The front-runner was Jules Ferry, but because he was the Opportunist

Republic incarnate, he aroused intense hostility. Crowds massed on the Place de la Concorde, whipped up by radicals, Boulangists, Blanquists and anarchists who threatened an insurrection in Paris if Ferry were elected. Radicals and conservatives had to agree on a candidate to keep out Ferry. Floquet was not acceptable to the conservatives; Freycinet was not acceptable to the radicals. They settled for an outsider, Sadi Carnot, who belonged to a dynasty of republican technicians, grandson of the 'organiser of victory' in the French revolutionary wars. Ferry himself was wounded a week later in an assassination attempt.

REVENGE OF THE DISINHERITED: BOULANGISM

The exclusion of Ferry did not satisfy radicals or conservatives for long. They wanted to have done with the Opportunist Republic. After the Wilson scandal and the fall of Grévy it seemed vulnerable; and in Boulanger they had a stick to beat it with. Boulanger was adopted as a champion by the disinherited on both Right and Left, although for some time the left hand did not know what the right was doing [45].

An early interest in Boulanger was shown by Bonapartists who had dropped the hereditary principle and accepted the Republic as a form of government, but wanted to revise the constitution. In particular, they wanted to establish the direct election of the president of the Republic; after all, that was how Louis-Napoleon had started in 1848. In January 1888 a Bonapartist journalist, Georges Thiébaud, introduced Boulanger to Prince Jérôme-Napoleon in Switzerland. Each denied that he was personally interested in running for the presidency, although the prince later admitted that Boulanger was 'a nail to hang your coat on' [46 *p. 96*]. Meanwhile a Bonapartist cable-magnate, Count Dillon, realized that they would have to look to the royalist camp for funds. For his part the Comte de Paris concluded that after a string of electoral defeats a plebiscite in the Bonapartist manner offered the best chance of success, appealing to the people over the heads of parties and politicians. Royalist leaders such as Mackau and Albert de Mun were ready to try Boulanger. The Duchesse d'Uzès, whom Boulanger as War Minister had once called on in order to apologize for a subordinate's refusal to allow her to hunt in the forest of Rambouillet, was happy to provide funds. As a later exposure of the affair had it, 'for the royalists the general is a card; for the general, royalism is a bank' [46 *p. 115*].

All these negotiations went on in the deepest secrecy. Publicly, Boulanger was seen to be a man of the Left. He was promoted by radicals and members of the extreme Left like the former Communard, Henri Rochefort. Déroulède's *Ligue des Patriotes* acted as an extra-parliamentary organization for Boulangism. In parliament, one of the radical Boulangists, Laguerre, demanded the revision of the constitution on 30 March. He provoked the fall of the ministry and its replacement by one under Floquet, who was known to favour revision. Boulanger was sent on a campaign of by-elections quite shamelessly as a media attraction. Under the list system a whole department had to be polled when one seat fell vacant. Boulanger presented his candidature, fought the election, resigned, and moved on to the next contest. He both seduced and repelled the Left. It was impossible to be sure what he stood for. He divided radicals, socialists and Blanquists down the middle: some issued grave warnings, others jumped on to the bandwagon. What was incontestable was his massive popular appeal. The socialist militants of Bordeaux, sensing the mood of the unemployed dock workers, threw in their lot with Boulanger. The support he received in the mining communities of the Nord department where he stood in April 1888 has been described as an 'explosion of working-class discontent' [47 *pp. 174–5*]. In the Isère, on the other hand, while the towns and industrial districts stayed republican, rural areas where Napoleon had been acclaimed on his return from Elba in 1815 rallied to Boulanger [48].

Gradually, rumours about the General's links with the Right leaked out. More and more activists on the Left worried that Boulanger would not make the Republic more responsive to the people but turn out to be a new Bonaparte. In May 1888 a Society of the Rights of Man was set up by a group of radicals, socialists and Opportunists to fight him. Clemenceau, changing his mind about Boulanger, joined it. In July, Boulanger decided to take up a seat in the Chamber and called for its dissolution. Floquet, the prime minister, attacked him for having 'passed from sacristies to the antechambers of princes' [49 *p. 402*]. Boulanger's republicanism was openly impugned. He challenged Floquet to a duel, but it was the white-haired premier who wounded the General in the throat.

These revelations made the conservatives happier with Boulanger, and they increased their support for him in a number of by-elections held in August. Republicans drew further back and attacked him as a reactionary and a Bonapartist. Boulanger replied to his accusers in a speech on the anniversary of Louis-Napoleon's *coup*, 2 December

1888. He was not a Bonapartist, he insisted, for Louis-Napoleon had restricted liberty and restored monarchical power. On the other hand, he favoured not an intransigent, closed Republic but 'a new, national Republic, open to all decent men' [*Doc. 7*]. This, in fact, was exactly what republicans feared: a hole punched in the principle of legitimacy which would end their monopoly of power and make way for a ruling majority in which the Right could participate.

Boulanger had one more chance. Floquet challenged him to fight a by-election in Paris in January 1889. Unfortunately, it was impossible to construct a complete republican alliance against Boulanger. The republican candidate represented the radicals and Opportunists but the socialists ran their own man and one wing of the Blanquists continued to support Boulanger in harness with the conservatives. Boulanger was thus able to draw support from the working-class suburbs of Paris as well as from the wealthy western districts, and he won the election.

The tolerance of the Third Republic could not be tried too far. A tough Minister of the Interior, Ernest Constans, determined to smash the Boulangist menace. The *Ligue des Patriotes*, which had organized the rank-and-file of Boulangism, was dissolved. Déroulède and Laguerre were prosecuted. Boulanger, Rochefort and Dillon, all of whom fled, were condemned *in absentia* by the Senate sitting as a High Court. The electoral system which had allowed Boulangism to flourish was altered: single-member constituencies were brought back in February 1889 and the right to stand in several constituencies at once was ended that August. In the elections of October 1889 monarchists freely ran Boulangists in the constituencies they could not win alone [50], but radicals now concluded that revision of the constitution played into the hands of the Right and sank their differences with the Opportunists. Monarchists, Bonapartists and Boulangists were all put in their place, with 210 seats to the republicans' 360. The Republic was secure for the moment, but a new force was emerging to cause concern: socialism.

4   SOCIAL STRUCTURE

The political system of the Third Republic cannot be studied in isolation from its social structure. Social strains or conflicts have immediate political repercussions. Land hunger in Russia, the declining petty bourgeoisie in Germany, and the toughness of the oligarchy in Spain were structural factors which in part explain the Revolution of 1917, the National Socialist seizure of power in 1933 and the Spanish Civil War. French society, partly because of the achievements of the Revolution of 1789, partly because of the slow, steady nature of its economic growth, was comparatively harmonious. It may be, to reverse the argument, that the very stability of French society permitted the luxury of sharp political divisions.

THE PEASANTRY

The countryside weighed heavily in French life. The total population in 1901 was 39 million, of whom 23 million lived in rural areas (defined as communes with an agglomerated population of under 2,000) and 16 million worked in agriculture. The pace of change was slow: in 1846 the rural population had been 27 million and the agricultural population 20 million, while as late as 1931 the rural population was 20 million and the agricultural population 11 million. Fears were expressed at the turn of the century about rural depopulation. In fact the countryside remained healthily populated; far more significant was the shift away from agricultural activity.

Social stratification in the countryside was far less sharp than in the countries of southern and eastern Europe. France was a country of small farms rather than of large estates and an agricultural proletariat. Properties under 5 hectares accounted for 71 per cent of properties and 14 per cent of the land surface in France in 1892, which may be compared with 54 per cent of properties and 6 per cent of the land surface in Hungary in 1895. France was to a large extent a rural democracy, with 75 per cent of properties in 1882 owner-occupied, while 6 per cent were under *métayage* (share-cropping, under which the farmer was provided by the landlord with seed, livestock and tools as well as land, and had to surrender half the crop), and 17 per cent were rented [51]. On the other hand the rented properties made up nearly half of the cultivated area, including the huge cereal and sugar-beet farms of the Paris basin and the north of France, owner-occupied farms were predominantly in the poorer upland regions, and in the Midi the development of wine monoculture in response to vastly increasing consumption after 1850 threw up a large winegrowing proletariat [52].

The opening up of agricultural land in Russia and the United States and the improvement of transport by steamship and railway lost one-quarter of the agricultural market to foreigners between 1877 and 1886 and drove down farm prices between 1875 and 1900 in France by 27 per cent for cereals and 19 per cent for meat. This reduced the capital value of land by (on average) one-third between 1879 and 1912. But the pressure was taken off tenant-farmers, who obtained lower rents and longer tenures (even if they were not indemnified for improvements made to the farm when they left or were evicted), and also off agricultural labourers and farm-hands, whose wages rose significantly at the end of the century. The agricultural interest secured protection against cheap imports of cereals, meat and wine under tariffs of 1885 and 1892. This spared them the need to modernize agriculture radically. On the other hand, there was some increase in agricultural productivity as a result of mechanization to save on expensive labour (threshing machines, horsedrawn reapers and, on the eve of the war, the first reaper-binders) and the use of chemical fertilizers to improve yields [53]. The decline of grain and meat prices and the growth of urban markets supplied by railway encouraged different forms of specialization. These included dairy farming (for milk, butter and cheese) in Normandy, Brittany, the Centre and Poitou-Charentes, sugar-beet in the North-East and wine along the Mediterranean coast [54]. The phylloxera epidemic of the 1880s destroyed most of the vines, but production recovered so rapidly after replanting that wine prices fell by 50 per cent between the 1880s and 1900–7 [55 *p. 299*].

One historian of this subject has called his book 'The Class Struggle in the Countryside' [56]. Certainly there were cases of rural strikes and unionization, notably of the woodcutters of the Centre in 1891–2, the winegrowing proletariat of the south in 1904 and 1907 and the *métayers* of the Allier (almost) in 1909. But several qualifications must be made. First, peasants as tenants and owners were far more concerned by prices and rents than by wages. The best way for peasants to cope with the problem of markets was to form co-operatives to buy seeds and fertilizers, to provide credit and insurance and to market their goods [57]. Second, rural hierarchies persisted, not least because co-operatives were often funded and taken over by land-owners, who insisted that they were the instruments of 'social peace' in the 'agricultural class' as a whole, as opposed to the class organizations of the towns. Finally, though peasants made up two-thirds of the electorate, the main political battle was between anticlericalism and clericalism, which obliged the rural populations to line up behind republican or Catholic-conservative notables, with little chance to air their own grievances. Republican notables set up their own federation to control rural organizations, the *Société nationale d'encouragement à l'Agriculture*, to vie with the royalist *Union centrale des Syndicats agricoles de France*, set up in 1886 [58].

WORKERS

The size of France's proletariat must be put in perspective [59]. The number of industrial workers increased between 1886 and 1911 from 3 million to 4.75 million but in 1911 the active industrial population was only 33 per cent of the total active population as against 41 per cent in agriculture. In 1870 the French working class was composed of two dominant elements. First, there was the artisan élite, the skilled craftsmen of the towns, owning or renting small workshops, with long years of apprenticeship behind them and often the sons and fathers of craftsmen in the same trade. Second there were the workers based in the countryside, such as miners, glass-workers or textile workers. Miners' leaders preserved the right to hire and pay their own teams, negotiating terms with the employer, and miners often retained small plots after (early) retirement [60]. Textile workers, such as the silk workers of the Isère, were overwhelmingly female, the menfolk concentrating on farming [61].

Widening markets for cheap, mass-produced goods were nevertheless undermining these structures. Larger factories were set up, particularly in newer industries such as chemicals, rubber and engineering, which were situated in the new suburbs of large cities rather than in traditional working-class districts. The mechanization of manufacturing processes from silk-weaving and watchmaking to boot and shoemaking took place later in France than in Great

Britain, and with painful results. Some skills were transferrable, so that the gunmakers of Saint-Étienne, undermined by Belgian arms manufacturers, took up bicycle-making and turned the town into a French Coventry [62]. Elsewhere, however, mechanization made craft-skills dispensable, cracked open the exclusiveness of trades and made it possible to replace highly paid workers with all-round skills by lower-paid semi-skilled workers who had only one specialized function to perform [63]. The expanding labour force was recruited from new sectors. Often it was drawn from rural industries which had been destroyed by the competition of more modern methods. Women, who were generally paid less that half the male wage, made up 30 per cent of the industrial workforce in 1866, rising to 37 per cent in 1906. They were also far more likely than British or German women to return to work after marriage and child-bearing.

Statistics for 1906 show that they were concentrated in the clothing industry (1.4 million women, 89 per cent of the workforce) and textiles (0.5 million, 56 per cent). This may be compared to domestic service (0.75 million, 77 per cent) and agriculture (3.3 million, 38 per cent of the workforce) [64]. The number of foreign immigrants – Belgians, in the textile conurbation of Lille-Roubaix-Tourcoing, joined towards the end of the century by Italians in the steelworks of Lorraine – reached 1,132,000 (2.8 per cent of the population) in 1911. Since the immigrants were ready to take low-paid jobs, they were often seen as a threat to the native workforce: a dozen Italians were killed at Aigues-Mortes on the Mediterranean coast in 1893. Since protection was less effective for industry than for agriculture, employers resorted to a wide range of techniques to   increase productivity and improve labour discipline. Hours were long (and a law of 1892 imposing an eleven hour day for women was widely flouted), piecework was introduced, the autonomy of miners' leaders was abolished, and in some single-industry towns the company, which generally ran the local council, provided housing, allotments, schools (run by religious congregations) and medical services the better to retain and control the workforce [65].

New kinds of labour organization had to be developed in order to defend workers' interests. Trade unions, which were properly authorized in 1884 (in the minds of the legislators to detach workers from militant agitators), were able to put up a united front to employers in order to improve or defend wages and conditions, using the threat of strike action. The strike tended to be used offensively, to improve wages, in boom periods, by (skilled) printers, metal-workers and building workers; and defensively, to defend wages, in times of depression, by the 'big battalions' of weavers and miners [66]. Unionization rather lagged behind strike activity. The proportions of workers in various industries unionized by 1912 were 32 per cent in mining, 30 per cent in building, 27 per cent in transport and only 13 per cent in textiles [67]. The total number in unions in 1913 was 1,027,000, which amounted to about 10 per cent of wage-earners, much less than the 26 per cent unionized in Great Britain. There were only 89,300 women in trade unions at that time, not least because men often organized to enforce a closed shop against unskilled labour and female labour, which were seen as a threat to the wages and jobs of skilled male workers [68].

A union set up by a particular trade in one town was liable to be extremely vulnerable. Regional and then national federations of category unions were therefore organized. A national federation was achieved by the printers in 1881, the builders in 1882, the railway workers in 1890, the miners (after one attempt in 1883) in 1890 and the textile workers in 1891. But France was a large country and industrial conditions varied a great deal from one end to the other. The moderate, well-organized miners of the Nord and Pas-de-Calais, for example, refused to go along with the militant miners of the Centre and Midi when the latter called a strike in 1902, and they made a separate peace with the authorities [69]. In general, unions federated into one body in a single town were far more effective than they were as members of category federations. This was the significance of the *Bourses du Travail*. These were labour exchanges, in which all local unions were represented, set up under the 1884 law to fight unemployment. They were subsidized by the municipality and could therefore afford to have one or two paid officials. In practice they were admirable unions of unions which founded new unions, increased the membership of old ones, amalgamated small craft-unions into larger industry-based ones, provided libraries for the self-education of the workforce and (not least) organized support among all unions for local strikes [70]. In 1892 ten *Bourses du Travail* formed a national federation, which rivalled the national federation of category unions – the *Confédération Générale du Travail*, or CGT, which was set up in 1895.

THE *PETITE BOURGEOISIE*

The *petite bourgeoisie*, known also as the *classes moyennes* and the 'new social strata' acclaimed by Gambetta, formed a thick wedge in

French society between the masses and the élite [71]. One gauge of its size was the 26 per cent of the active population engaged in commerce, banking, transport and services in 1911 (the proportion in Italy at the same time was only 16 per cent). Broadly speaking, the *petite bourgeoisie* could be divided into two sorts: *la boutique*, or the small employers in commerce and industry, who had some capital but little education, and the white-collar workers (clerks or lower civil servants), who had some education but little or no capital.

The small employers were often themselves of popular origin. Miners dismissed for radical activities regularly became bar-owners. Peasants from the Auvergne formed a colony of 75,000 in Paris in the 1890s, making a living as rag-and-bone men or wine- and coal-merchants. In 1911, two in five Auvergnats in Paris were tradesmen, and every tenth tradesman and fifth café or hotel owner was an Auvergnat (or Auvergnate) [72]. After 1880 the competition from large firms and department stores made life difficult for small tradesmen, and the Bretons who migrated to Paris at the end of the century were forced to find work as domestic servants or as labourers in railway yards, gasworks or tanning factories. On the other hand, urbanization created new clienteles. While the number of grocers in the smart 1st *arrondissement* of Paris fell from 131 to 60 between 1860 and 1914, squeezed out by the department stores, they rose from 196 to 456 in the working-class 20th *arrondissement* [73].

Shopkeeping was an unstable occupation but it was a good starting-point for employment in the more stable white-collar world. Social mobility was promoted by a number of factors. As children became less of an asset (as cheap labour) and more of a liability, so stricter birth-control was practised, pressing down the birth rate at the end of the century. This took place in the town before the country, and among the petty bourgeoisie before the working class. In the absence of National Insurance and a Welfare State the saving classes were sharply divided from the spending classes. The petty bourgeoisie were notoriously provident, putting their money into voluntary schemes to insure against sickness and old-age and to pay for a decent funeral. Above all there was the channel of education. After 1881 both elementary and higher primary education were free, but the desire to send children out to work early had to be balanced against the multiplication of jobs available to girls as well as boys who had some educational attainment. Between 1871 and 1912, for example, the number of posts in banking, shipping and insurance and on the railways increased from 71,000 to 310,000, those in the post office from 34,000 to 120,000, and those in public education from 110,000 to 180,000. The proportion of women in banking and commerce rose from 26 per cent in 1866 to 41 per cent in 1911. There were 13,000 female clerks, stenographers, typists and telephonists in the post office in 1913. Laicization created posts in teaching and nursing which had previously been occupied by nuns. However, women accounted for only 8 per cent of pharmacists, 3 per cent of doctors and 0.3 per cent of lawyers in 1906.

The wages of clerks and minor civil servants lagged a long way behind their status, and while the professional organization of white-collar workers in the private sector was fairly strong, in the public sector it was contested by the authorities. This was especially the case when civil service unions sought affiliation to the *Bourses du Travail* or CGT, which were considered to be revolutionary, or went on strike. When post office workers went on strike in 1909, for example, 500 of them were sacked [74].

THE ÉLITE

The social élite in France included components of birth, wealth and education. The promotional power of education was a seductive myth, and was given practical reinforcement by the military service law of 1889, which exempted from two of the three years' service anyone with a degree from a faculty or diploma from a *grande école*. As a result the university population leaped from 17,000 in 1888 to 27,000 in 1896. However, careers were far from automatically open to talent. The *baccalauréat* or secondary school leaving certificate was required to enter a faculty (and hence the professions), but secondary education, even in the state sector, was fee-paying. There were very few scholarships, and these usually went to the sons of civil servants. An education in Greek and Latin (not the newer, modern education) was needed to get into a law or medical faculty until 1902, and the general cultural skills required tended to penalise pupils from working-class backgrounds and women, at least until 1902, when the non-classical *baccalauréat* became an option [75]. Regional universities were founded after 1893 but Paris was still the place to go to (in 1914 52 per cent of French medical students and 46 per cent of law and arts students were at Paris University), and this pushed up the cost of education still further [76]. With no other capital but cultural, a scholarship boy might expect to enter an arts faculty or the *École Normale Supérieure* in Paris and pursue a career in the University, with the status of a civil servant, as a *lycée* teacher or academic. Another route for those who excelled in mathematics was recruitment by competitive examination into *grandes écoles* such as the *École Polytechnique*, which existed alongside the universities. This was the gateway to top posts in the army, civil service and nationalized industries such as the mines (graduates of Polytechnique rarely patronized private industry before 1890). Though schools of business and applied sciences were developing, they were not a necessary condition of success in business. New entrepreneurs were still able to make their fortunes in new industries, as the Lumière brothers did in the electricity industry or the Renault brothers in automobiles. Otherwise the *patronat* of provincial family firms was well established, and produced the next generation of owners and managers from its own heirs [77; 78].

The secret weapon that ensured the continuity of the bourgeoisie was the *patrimoine* or family inheritance, which took the form of stocks and shares, urban property, and even land [79]. It provided the capital for the family business, and for the prospering of the family by wise investments in new joint-stock companies and government bonds, both French and foreign. It afforded the cost of education for rich heirs who attended law faculties and went on to monopolize élite posts in politics, the magistracy, administration and diplomatic corps [80]. One of the outstanding features of the French élite at the turn of the century and one which made it distinct from the German élite was the interlocking of the official and business sectors. This was established by growing rates of intermarriage between families of high officials and big businessmen, by invitations to high officials to sit on the boards of railway companies and banks, and by the resignation of officials in mid-career to accept management positions in private firms, a system known as *pantouflage* [81; 82].

As for the French nobility, it was not what it had been before 1789 but it was still a significant force. Its corporate privileges, such as the right to monopolize a second chamber, had long been abolished and it would thus be more correct to speak of 5,000 noble families rather than of a nobility. Though the 1870s were dubbed the 'Republic of dukes', nobles were virtually excluded from political office after 1879, and their representation in the Chamber of Deputies declined from 34 per cent in 1871 to 9 per cent in 1914. On the other hand, nobles were the dominant influence in polite society, through the salons of the likes of Madame de Loynes in the Faubourg Saint-Germain, which did the honours of a court, and the governing bodies of sport, such as the Jockey Club. They were no longer only a landed aristocracy, but had considerable resources in urban property and share capital: 27 per cent of the directors of railway companies and 22 per cent of those of insurance companies were noble in 1900. Noble families were also keen to marry their daughters (rather than their sons) into new wealth. The industrialist Eugène Schneider married his four daughters into the nobility. Winaretta Singer, whose American father made a fortune from the invention of the sewing machine, married Prince Edmond de Polignac and became a leading society hostess. The monied bourgeoisie and the landed aristocracy amalgamated very much as a single plutocracy. This did not mean that there were no tensions in the upper echelons of society between parvenus and established nobles, provincial and Parisian nobles and pre-Revolution and imperial nobles. But the issue was one of snobbery rather than of substance.

5 SOCIALISM

French socialism in this period, though sharing the common aim of the collectivization of large-scale industry, was sharply divided over strategy. In the first place, it was debated whether the labour movement should be led by a socialist party which sought state power in order to bring about socialist society by a wave of nationalizations, or whether it should remain apart from parties and politicians, even socialist ones. In this case it would rely on the trade unions and look to abolish the state, founding a socialist society of autonomous trade unions freely federating together. Secondly, so far as socialist parties were concerned, it was debated whether they should achieve state power by revolution, or legally, through the electoral system.

These debates reflected a rivalry in French socialism of two traditions. On the one hand, there was the anarchist gospel of Pierre-Joseph Proudhon, who had died in 1865 but inspired the French sections and trade unions affiliated to the First Workers' International (1864–77), the Internationalists who formed a narrow majority on the Paris Commune, and after its suppression the so-called anti-authoritarian International which recognized the autonomy of sections and federations and was based on the Jura Federation in Switzerland. On the other hand, there was the socialist gospel of Karl Marx, who inspired the British, Belgian and German affiliates of the International, and tried to impose a centralized discipline on the International through its General Council in London [83]. The second debate, between revolution and legalism, reflected a wider ambiguity in French society. France, of course, had a famous revolutionary tradition, honoured by the events of 1789, 1830, 1848 and 1871. But that revolutionary tradition had borne fruit, and France, uniquely in Europe, was a democratic Republic. Whether that Republic should be dismissed as simply another weapon of the bourgeois state, or whether it should be used as the vessel into which socialist waters could be poured, was a recurrent issue within French socialism [84].

PARTY AND CLASS: POLITICAL ACTION AND DIRECT ACTION

The crushing of the Paris Commune in 1871 effectively destroyed socialist organization in France for a decade. Workers were minded to steer clear of the dangerous reefs of politics and to regard themselves only as producers. When workers' congresses met in Paris in 1876, Lyon in 1878 and Marseille in 1879 only working men were permitted to speak and vote, and there was to be no discussion of politics. However, Jules Guesde, a former anarchist of the Jura Federation who had been converted to Marxism in 1876 by German *émigrés* in Paris, was keen to organize the working class into a political party, regardless of the political preferences of its individual members. He claimed that this would be a party unlike other parties, serving the interests of the workers themselves, not the ambitions of the party leaders.

The French Workers' Party (POF) was duly launched at the third workers' congress in Marseille in 1879 [85; 86]. At the outset only a fraction of the working class was represented – hatters and shoe-makers, but not weavers, miners or foundry workers. Moreover the very different opinions within this artisan élite could not be reconciled. Disagreement led first to the breakaway from the POF of anarchists such as Jean Grave, a Parisian shoemaker who disliked the constraints of any party and said that he preferred dynamite to the ballot box [1881], then to criticisms of Guesde by Paul Brousse, and anarchist member of the International who had been involved in an attempt to seize the town hall of Barcelona during the Spanish Republic. Brousse argued that the wholesale nationalizations demanded by Guesde would reinforce state power and engender a socialist dictatorship, and proposed instead that municipalities should be freed from the centralized state and be liberated to municipalize local services such as gas and water in a new version of the anarchist 'propaganda by deed'. In addition, he attacked the authoritarian model of the party imposed by Guesde, who had gone to London and consulted only with Marx and his French son-in-law, Paul Lafargue, when drafting the first electoral manifesto, arguing that each regional federation of the party should be able to draft its own manifesto. Brousse and the anti-Marxists won a majority against the Guesdists at the 1882 party congress, and formed their own party, the Federation of Socialist Workers of France (FTSF) [87].

In the early 1880s France was hit by depression and

unemployment and working-class discontent increased. A large demonstration of the unemployed took place in Paris in March 1883 and a long strike, studied by Émile Zola for his novel *Germinal*, broke out in the mines of Anzin in February 1884. A mass base for socialism was taking shape. To prevent this, the Opportunist oligarchy decided in March 1884 to authorize trade unions fully. If unions were legal, it was argued, moderate workers would join them and they would no longer be the vehicle of extremists. Moreover, if the working class was able to improve its wages and conditions by bargaining, it would be less vulnerable to the blandishments of 'outside' socialist agitators. The government made sure of this by requiring unions to submit their statutes and the names of their officers to the authorities and by confining them to the pursuit of economic interests. The emancipated trade unions, however, were seen by socialists as too rich a prize to be passed up. Jules Guesde set up a National Federation of Trade Unions in 1886, in order to gear as many trade unions as possible to Marxist ideology and to the strategy of the conquest of political power by the Parti Ouvrier. He was particularly successful among the textile workers of northern France, where party and unions worked hand in glove, the militants of one generally being the militants of the other [88].

Meanwhile Brousse and his Federation of Socialist Workers, despite their anarchist origins, came to be known as the Possibilists, because of their keenness to come to power at a local level first, should that be possible, and because they soon became involved in the wheeling and dealing of party politics. They won nine seats on the Paris municipal council in 1887, entered alliances with the ruling radicals, and opposed the navvies' strike of 1888. This disgusted Jean Allemane, who was an associate of Brousse, but had been deported for his activities during the Commune and had retained the intransigence of the Communards. His support lay among unskilled rather than skilled workers, who followed Brousse. From the premiss that 'the emancipation of the working class *can only* be by the workers themselves' [89 *p. 45*], he argued that their weapon must be the general strike, which would result in the transfer of workshops and work-sites to workers' associations. His supporters broke with the Possibilists in 1890 and set up the Revolutionary Socialist Workers' Party. This captured the Paris *Bourse du Travail* from the Possibilists in 1891 and the following year organized a National Federation of *Bourses* [90]. A bid was then made to break the hold of the Guesdists on the trade unions. In this the Allemanists were joined by the founders of the *Bourse* of St Nazaire, a young lawyer, Aristide Briand, and a journalist, Fernand Pelloutier, who also favoured the general strike [91]. The Guesdists were opposed to the general strike because it erupted beyond their control and did not help the party to achieve political power. But Briand was able to obtain the support of the majority of delegates at the congress of the National Federation of Trade Unions at the end of 1894 for the general strike. The way was now open for the formation of a new federation, the General Confederation of Labour (CGT), which was inspired by the anarchist and Allemanist strategy of the general strike. This operated in tandem with the Federation of *Bourses du Travail*, of which Pelloutier became secretary in 1895.

REVOLUTION OR REFORM?

Whether the Paris Commune was a proletarian revolution has long been debated by historians, but for Guesde and the French Workers' Party it was an article of faith. They made a cult of the Commune as a class war, highlighting less the insurrection of 18 March 1871 than the brutal repression by the bourgeois state of the *Semaine Sanglante* at the end of May. On 23 May 1880 Guesde led a march of 25,000 to the *Mur des Fédérés* of the Père Lachaise cemetery in eastern Paris, where the Communards had made a last stand, been massacred and shovelled into communal graves [92]. This event, which became an annual pilgrimage, was followed by a boycott of the celebrations of 14 July 1880, organized by the republican government. The message to workers was that they were members of a pariah class, excluded from the political nation, and that the Republic, despite the rhetoric of rights of man and the revolutionary tradition, concealed the mailed fist of the bourgeoisie which was prepared to resort to state terror when necessary. Since the Republic was a class state, rigged to further the interests of the bourgeoisie, the working class had no alternative but to organize to seize state power from them by revolutionary means.

This reasoning was shared by those professionals of revolution, the Blanquists, whose leaders (Édouard Vaillant, Émile Eudes, Ernest Granger) were former Communards who returned under the amnesty of 1880 and set up a Central Revolutionary Committee, named after the Parisian organization responsible for the popular revolution of 31 May 1793 [93]. And yet both Blanquists and Guesdists could not fail to realize that France was now not a dictatorship but a democratic republic, with elections held under universal suffrage and governments responsible to parliamentary majorities.

To demand an amnesty for the Communards, the aged Blanqui stood in an election at Bordeaux in 1879 (which was annulled) and again at Lyon in 1880 (in which he was defeated). Vaillant was elected to the Paris municipal council in 1884. The Guesdists participated in the elections of 1881, with a minimum programme designed to draw votes from the radicals while keeping their maximum programme up their sleeves. The only logic of their position was that the revolution was a code for class war, and that class war was preached to forge the class consciousness of working men and persuade them to vote for the Workers' Party, not for any other republican (or non-republican) candidate.

The other issue that soon confronted French socialists was that of the Republic. How should they act if the Republic was seen to be in danger, as during the Boulanger affair? As workers voted with enthusiasm for Boulanger, Lafargue threw in his lot with Boulangism as an attack on the bourgeois Republic, Guesde struggled to keep the Workers' Party neutral, and the Blanquists were divided, with Granger seeing the opportunity to mobilize the people of Paris for an insurrectionary adventure, while Vaillant feared the general as a new dictator and turned against him. The Possibilists joined the Society of Rights of Man to fight Boulanger, while Benoît Malon, a former Communard and Possibilist and editor of the ecumenical *Revue socialiste*, wrote early in 1889 that 'the democratic and progressive Republic is the basis of our action, and we must be prepared to defend it against reactionaries as well as against its dubious saviours' [94 *p. 223*]. This was a powerful argument for many socialists. For them the Republic was not a class state but the framework within which they must operate: destruction of the Republic by reactionaries or demagogues would end the liberties which allowed the labour movement and socialist parties to flourish. The lesson of antisocialist laws current in the German Reich was only too clear. Moreover, the Republic was based on the revolutionary principles of the rights of man. Political rights had been granted in universal suffrage, but social rights were also implied and remained to be actualized. The task of socialists was to add social rights to political rights, to convert the democratic Republic into the democratic *and social* Republic.

Not only was revolution superfluous in a democratic Republic, but it became clear that where authoritarian methods were resorted to by government and employers, far from gagging legal and democratic socialism, they could be turned to its advantage. May Day demonstrations in favour of an eight-hour day were proposed by the Second International of national socialist parties that was founded in Paris in 1889 and taken up by the Guesdist Workers' Party as preferable to strike action. On May Day 1891, however, demonstrators in the northern woollen town of Fourmies were shot at by the military, leaving nine dead, eight of them youths [95]. Paul Lafargue was imprisoned for a year for inciting disorder there, but far from calling for revolution, the Guesdists campaigned to have Lafargue elected to parliament for Lille in a by-election six months later [96]. Alexander Millerand, a lawyer and radical deputy who had defended Lafargue at his trial, was so incensed by the state's violence against the labour movement that he converted to socialism [97; 98]. Again, in May 1892, the miners and glassworkers of Carmaux took over the municipality from the mine-owners' representatives and elected a miner mayor. The mine-owners, headed by the Marquis de Solages, refused the miner leave to serve as mayor, whereupon the miners launched a successful three-month strike, the Marquis was forced to resign as deputy, and in the by-election of January 1893 the miners elected Jean Jaurès, a professor from the university of Toulouse and hitherto a radical, as their socialist deputy [99; 100].

The electoral success of the socialists continued. In the municipal elections of May 1892 they gained a majority on 23 councils. This made it possible to find employment in town-hall administration for militants who had lost their jobs in workshops and factories. In the parliamentary elections of 1893, shortly after troops were sent in to close the *Bourse du Travail* of Paris, which was considered a hive of revolutionary activity, the socialists increased their tally from 12 to 48 seats; a 'red belt' began to take shape in the Paris suburbs [101] Guesde was himself elected in the northern textile town of Roubaix and tried to justify his success by arguing that electoral action was still revolutionary, both because the goal of a socialist society was revolutionary and because it simply translated class war into a mass vote [*Doc. 8a*].

While revolution was now no more than rhetoric, class war was also thrown into doubt. For although socialist parties converted middle-class intellectuals such as Millerand and Jaurès, they were essentially proletarian parties, and as proletarian parties found their electorate limited by the size of the proletariat. In order to win a majority they would increasingly be obliged to make alliances with bourgeois republicans [102].

The strength of Guesde's Workers' Party, for instance, was in large-scale industry which had a well-defined proletariat, especially in smallish single-industry towns such as Roubaix (textiles), Troyes (stocking-weaving) and Montluçon (iron founding). However, in large towns with highly-differentiated populations in which the proletariat was far from being a majority, such as Lille, the Guesdists had to co-operate with the radicals in order to win the town in 1896. The Guesdists were basically a working-class party, but it was not impossible for them to gain support in the countryside. This was easiest where class tensions were sharp, as in the Allier, where 29 per cent of the party membership in 1894–9 were *métayers* or other peasants [103]. Communal traditions in the countryside – forest rights or the right to graze livestock on the stubble – gave some purchase to socialist missionaries, but they had to be cautious with such terms as 'collectivism', saying that they meant co-operatives or the ownership of forests by communes, not any threat to private property. In the Midi, where class tensions were more diffuse than in the north, there was a vigorous Montagnard or social-democratic tradition going back to 1849–52. This could be exploited by socialists after 1880, though they had to remember that in the South socialism meant protest, not Marxism [104]. The Workers' Party duly supported the radical-socialist doctor, Ernest Ferroul, in his capture of the municipality of Narbonne in 1888, while in the parliamentary elections of 1898 socialist federations in the Midi (in spite of orders from Paris) sought alliances with radical-socialists from the first ballot.

In the Chamber of Deputies there were also pressures on socialists to reach agreement with bourgeois radicals. After 1893 there were fifty socialists in the Chamber, including 'independent' socialists such as Millerand and Jaurès who had been elected on another ticket and then switched to socialism. Socialists collaborated in the Chamber with radicals against the authoritarian measures of the government. They supported the radical ministry of Léon Bourgeois in 1895–6. After socialist success in the municipal elections of 1896, Millerand proposed a programme at St Mandé outside Paris which he hoped would unite all socialists and make way for electoral alliances with radicals in 1898. It was a very dilute programme: the acquisition of power by universal suffrage (not by revolution), the gradual transfer of private to social property and a balance between international commitment and patriotism. However, it remained to be seen how far along the road radicals – popularly described as having their hearts on the left and wallets on the right – were prepared to go. Collaboration to defend the republican form could easily give way to disagreement about content.

ANARCHISM AND ANARCHO-SYNDICALISM

Those anarchists who had flirted with the Workers' Party, as we have seen, did not stay long with it. Jean Grave left in 1881, Sébastien Faure, the Jesuit-educated son of a Bordeaux merchant, broke with it in 1888. Others who had found their way into the Possibilist party left with Jean Allemane in 1890. Émile Pouget, who had had to interrupt his studies after his father's death and worked in a Paris department store, launched a scurrilous paper, *Père Peinard*, in 1889 [105]. Anarchists were generally individualists, ill at ease with the discipline of any political party or trade union. They regarded politicians – even socialist ones – as treacherous and trade unions as dedicated to narrow corporative interests. They tended to be self-educated artisans or *déclassé* intellectuals, locked into boring clerical jobs. They were opposed not only to economic exploitation but to all forms of oppression and were invariably hostile to the Church, the army, the police, the courts, the education system, parliament and government as well as to the capitalist system [106; 107].

On the same day as the massacre at Fourmies, anarchists waving red flags joined May Day demonstrators at Clichy, a suburb of Paris. Shots were exchanged and arrests made. The prosecution demanded the death penalty for the three accused. In the event the maximum sentence passed was five years. But Ravachol, a common law murderer and thief who escaped to Paris, set off bombs in the apartment blocks of the judges who had sentenced the Clichy anarchists. He was executed in July 1892, brazenly abusing authority and religion at the scaffold, and at once became a popular hero. On 9 December 1893 Auguste Vaillant (not the Blanquist), who had failed to make his fortune in Argentina, threw a bomb into the Chamber of Deputies. No one was killed, but he was duly executed. A week after the execution a bomb was thrown into the Café Terminus of St Lazare Station. The perpetrator was Émile Henry, a youth of 21, son of a Communard who had fled to Spain and been condemned to death in his absence. Henry had just failed to get into the *École Polytechnique*. He was entranced by Souvarine, the Russian anarchist of Zola's *Germinal*, and sympathized with the striking miners of Carmaux (his first bomb had been planted at the Paris offices of the Carmaux mining company). But he felt that all idle bourgeois were a legitimate target; hence his choice of a station restaurant [*Doc. 8b*]. Henry was executed in May 1894. President Carnot, who had pardoned none of the anarchists, was assassinated at Lyon a month later.

In February and July 1894 emergency legislation – nicknamed the *lois scélérats* (villainous laws) – was passed in an attempt to gag anarchist conspiracy and propaganda, and a trial of thirty anarchists including Grave and Faure was held in August. The trial was a fiasco. The defendants were acquitted and the anarchist press was reborn. Grave founded *Les Temps nouveaux*, Faure launched *Le Libertaire* with the former Communard Louise Michel, and Pouget restarted *Père Peinard*. But Fernand Pelloutier, secretary of the Federation of *Bourses du Travail*, argued that the time had come for the anarchists to put away their bombs and to make common cause with the labour movement, now that it had reasserted its independence of socialist parties and committed itself to the general strike. In his pamphlet *What is the General Strike?*, published in 1895, Pelloutier announced that the general strike guaranteed the success of the proletarian revolution, since it would force the military to disperse its efforts and could seize control of key services. He also wrote an open letter to anarchists, published in *Les Temps nouveaux* (November 1895), pointing out that the trade unions were no longer committed to narrow corporative interests or nurseries for aspiring deputies, but, especially through the *Bourses du Travail*, were the schools of the proletariat and the cells of the new socialist society, which would be 'a free association of free producers' [108]. Many anarchists, who had reason to consider the inadequacy of the individualist method, and who were excluded from the Second Socialist International by the Marxists in 1893 and 1896 for refusing to endorse political action, decided to reply positively to Pelloutier's invitation. Paul Delesalle, who worked on *Les Temps nouveaux*, became assistant secretary to Pelloutier on the Federation of *Bourses* in 1897 [109], while in 1900 Pouget became editor of the new CGT paper, *La Voix du Peuple*. The combination of anarchism and trade-unionism became a powerful cocktail: anarcho-syndicalism.

6 A CONSERVATIVE REPUBLIC?

The organization of the labour movement and socialism represented a new political menace. After 1890 it was in the interest of the French ruling class to sink its differences about religion and the constitution and organize itself in the defence of private property. The difficulty was that the republican regime – the only one among the major European states – was still contested; and the struggle to keep the republicans out of power in the 1870s had hardened the republicans in power against sharing it with anyone else. The principle of republican legitimacy and the requirements of social order were at odds with one another. Nevertheless there were attempts in the 1890s to sidestep political obstacles and construct a united ruling class on other bases.

ECONOMIC PROTECTION

World competition, falling prices for industrial goods, raw materials and foodstuffs, and declining rents and land values excited a drive for protection among agricultural and certain industrial interests. Outside parliament the Society of Agriculturalists and the Association of French Industry, which represented textiles and iron and steel, forged an alliance in 1889, with their eyes on the revision of the tariff due in 1892. The elections of October 1889 were a blow to the Right – not least to those who had flirted with Boulangism – and many conservatives now concluded that their main interest lay not in trying to change the constitution but in pooling their resources with property-owners in general and pushing for protection. The aim was not just to safeguard sales and investments, but to stabilize the countryside, reduce the rural depopulation which gave rise to unemployment and social conflict in the towns, and to organize the possessing classes in response to the organization of the labouring classes. Two months after the elections, in December 1889, an all-party agricultural protection group formed in the Chamber of Deputies, three or four hundred strong, under the presidency of Jules Méline, who had been responsible for the tariff of 1885. A similar all-party industrial protection group was also founded.

It remained to be seen whether the protectionist alliance could be converted into political capital. In March 1890 a former Boulangist, Jacques Piou, gathered together a Constitutional Right group based in the north of France which not only favoured protection but was also prepared to accept the Republic. Unfortunately it included only sixteen deputies. The vast majority of the Right was protectionist, but saw no question of abandoning the monarchy. The most that can be said is that the tariff that went through in 1892, baptized the Méline tariff, reconciled as many of the conflicting interests of the possessing classes as possible. It was heavily but not purely protectionist, making strategic exceptions where necessary [110; 111]. Conservatives were induced to live within the Republican church, although they could not be brought to the altar.

THE *RALLIEMENT*

The religious question, and in particular the school question, sharply divided Catholic conservatives from republicans. The Catholic Church was seen to have supported fallen monarchies and more recently the authoritarian Empire and the Moral Order regime of 1873–7. At the same time religion could be seen as a reinforcement of the social order, and after 1890 social order was at a premium. Many republicans were prepared to admit that the lay laws were too harsh, especially in the case of the education of girls, and that the attempt to replace the catechism in state schools by a code of secular morality had been a failure. Moderate conservatives like Jacques Piou were anxious to take advantage of what might be a disaggregation of the republican camp. He particularly hated the radicals, who since 1885 had been in a position to dictate anticlerical measures to the Opportunists. But Opportunists such as Étienne Lamy were willing to relax the lay laws, and it was Piou's strategy to accept the Republic in order to displace the radicals and form a new government majority composed of Opportunists and the moderate Right [112].

Before French Catholics would endorse the Republic in any numbers, a green light was required from the Papacy. If only for diplomatic reasons, this light was forthcoming. The Papacy was on bad terms with Italy since unification had absorbed the Papal States, and since 1888 Pope Leo XIII had been on bad terms with Germany. He needed the support of the French state to end his diplomatic isolation, and therefore French Catholics must reconcile themselves to the Republic. To test opinion Pope Leo spoke through Cardinal Lavigerie, Archbishop of Algiers. At a banquet on 12 November 1890 Lavigerie told naval officers of the French Mediterranean squadron that when a country was on the brink of an abyss (by which he understood socialism) and only unreserved support for the government of that country could save it, then that support was necessary. He then gave a toast to the French Republic [113].

This gesture was intolerable to die-hard royalists. The Republic was unacceptable not only because it was a republic, but because it was so incorrigibly anticlerical. The message went out from a royalist meeting in Nîmes that even if the republican door were opened the republicans would 'make the door so low that we would have to get on to our stomachs to pass through it' [114]. It was one thing to snub Lavigerie, another to snub the Pope. But true-blue royalists were simply not prepared to sacrifice their royalism to their Catholicism. Pope Leo made his views clear in his encyclical *Inter innumeras* of February 1892. He distinguished the constitution of a country, which was fixed, from its laws, which were not, and he urged French Catholics to accept the one and strive to change the other. Albert de Mun was happy to bow to the encyclical, and accept the Republic, but he found the doors of the royalist salons closed in his face. Only in economically advanced areas like the North, where social conflict was bitter and the nobility weak, did royalists rally to the Republic as instructed [115]. In more backward regions such as the West and Midi, where social conflict was less pronounced, the nobility was entrenched, and the Republic had been resisted by counter-revolution and White Terror for a century, the *Ralliement* was a total failure.

To be fair, the *Ralliement* was superfluous so long as the Opportunist governing oligarchy, which had survived Boulangism, remained in place. After 1890, however, Opportunists came under attack from former Boulangists who were now taking up anti-Semitism as a stick with which to beat what they called the 'Jewish party'. Maurice Barrès, a young journalist, stood as an anti-Semite at Nancy in the parliamentary elections of October 1889, having calculated that anti-Semitism had electric force as a popular protest against capitalist exploitation and political manipulation [116]. Édouard Drumont, who had published the best-selling *La France juive* in 1886, helped to found a French

National Anti-Semitic League which had a former Boulangist elected to parliament in 1890 [117]. Drumont soon launched an anti-Semitic paper, *La Libre Parole*, which scored a direct hit on the Opportunist oligarchy in November 1892 with the exposure of the Panama scandal. The Panama company, thirsty for finance to build its canal, and requiring a law to authorize a share-issue, used a pair of Jewish agents – the Frankfurt banker Jacques de Reinach and Cornelius Herz – to bribe ministers and deputies in order to have the law pushed through in 1888. The exposure of these dealings set back the careers of Rouvier and Clemenceau, ruined those of Floquet and Freycinet, and ended the Opportunist golden age of 1879–93. Jacques de Reinach committed suicide [118; 119; 120].

France was then on the eve of elections. The discrediting of republicans in general and Opportunists in particular reopened the way to a new government majority which included *Ralliés*. The indefatigable Jacques Piou urged this course in a *Figaro* article of January 1893: the majority must include all those who were dedicated to 'an open, tolerant, and honest Republic' [*Doc. 9a*]. In anticipation he renamed his Constitutional Right the Republican Right. However, the new Prime Minister, Charles Dupuy, a former Education Minister and uncompromised in the Panama episode, stuck rigidly to the canon of republican legitimacy. He took four radicals into his cabinet with a view to a 'republican concentration' at the elections, and in a speech at Toulouse in May 1893 firmly rejected Piou's approach [*Doc. 9b*]. Dupuy went into the elections of August–September 1893 alongside the radicals. Many *Ralliés* made their point by withdrawing at the second ballot, and instructing their followers to support a moderate republican against a socialist, but the compliment was rarely repaid by republicans. As a result the *Ralliés* lost heavily: only 36 out of 94 candidates were elected, and de Mun and Piou were among those defeated. Étienne Lamy also lost. On the other hand the radicals did well and the socialists quadrupled their tally to 48 seats.

SOCIAL REFORM

The economic and political orthodoxy in the 1880s endorsed free market capitalism, private property and minimal interference of the state in tackling social problems. One of its gurus, Paul Leroy-Beaulieu, who combined a huge private fortune with contributions to the establishment's *Revue des Deux Mondes* and lecturing to high civil servants at the *École Libre des Sciences*

Politiques, published an Essay on the *Distribution of Wealth and on the Trend to Decreasing Social Inequality* in 1881, in which he argued that capitalism was benefiting workers as much as capitalists and that the state was ill-advised to interfere in the operation of beneficial economic laws [121]. The orthodox view was that poverty should be dealt with not by the state but by the private provision of working people themselves, saving money against hard times through mutual insurance societies, and *in extremis* by the charity of the Christian churches.

This confidence, however, seemed to fly in the face of the deep economic depression of 1873–95, the rapid growth of the urban population, rising unemployment, the development of social scourges such as alcoholism, which was seen to be a peculiarly working-class vice [122], and the emergence of socialist parties and anarchism which appeared all the more threatening in the context of the Paris Commune. Organizations were duly set up to investigate social problems and to make proposals about social reform which modified the tenets of market capitalism and liberalism. These included the Musée social, an institute for social research and conference centre, founded in 1894, and the National League against Alcoholism, founded in 1895. These organizations were privately funded, but drew together a cross-section of the political élite, both Catholics and Protestants, republicans and royalists, paternalists and liberals with a social conscience. The same names appear on the roll call of founders, notable Émile Cheysson, a conservative technocrat who had developed company paternalism as managing director of the Le Creusot ironworks after 1871, and Jules Siegfried, a Protestant cotton importer of Le Havre, while the galaxy of honorary patrons included Jules Méline, Léon Bourgeois and René Waldeck-Rousseau [123].

Jules Siegfried, as a senator, sat on parliamentary commissions for public health and social insurance, but the enactment of reforms proved very difficult in the face of the prevailing orthodoxy. A law of 1892 established a maximum working day for women over eighteen, but adult males were expected to fend for themselves. In 1893 free medical aid was guaranteed for the poor, but towns which made their own provisions were allowed to opt out of the scheme, and all discussion of retirement pensions had to be abandoned to ensure the passage of the bill [124]. The cost of pensions implied income tax, which in turn meant an inquisition by the state into the financial affairs of the bourgeoisie, and any suggestion of income tax was furiously opposed. Léon Bourgeois became prime minister at the head of a radical cabinet which enjoyed the support of the socialists and boasted a broad programme of social reform. This included further limitation of the working day, accident insurance to be paid for by employers and pensions to be paid for by both employers and employees, complete freedom of association for trade unions and the compulsory arbitration of labour disputes. In addition, the burden of taxation was to be moved from the poor to the rich by a shift from indirect to direct taxation, in particular by the introduction of a graduated income tax and inheritance tax.

Bourgeois and the radicals were in no sense collectivist: they believed that the possession of private property was a precondition of liberty and that capitalism was the best way to create wealth. But updating the republican principle of fraternity, they developed the idea of Solidarism according to which those who took more out of society in terms of profits and dividends than others had a debt to society which had to be repaid in tax if social justice was to be ensured and class conflict avoided [125; 126; 127]. The menace of income tax, and the feeling that the Bourgeois cabinet was a hostage of the socialists, split the moderate republicans, now ironically known as Progressists, away from the radicals. Even in alliance with the conservatives the Progressists were in a minority in the Chamber, so they resorted to the Senate, which brought down the ministry by refusing to vote its credits.

The cabinet of Jules Méline which now took office was one of the longest-lasting before the war, in power from April 1896 until May 1898. It was a moderate republican ministry which survived with the votes of the Right, which was strictly against the rules of republican legitimacy. Radicals and socialists immediately challenged it on the grounds that it had a majority of republicans against it. The significant thing is that Méline did not deny the importance of the rules. Speaking in October 1897 he tried to turn them to his advantage. He argued that without the socialists the radicals would themselves be in a republican minority (and by implication that socialists were as unrepublican as the Right). Moreover he concentrated on the question of measures, not men. The ministry did not intend to declare war on religion, he said, but he underlined that 'our policy is republican, clearly republican' [*Doc. 10*]. The bill on industrial accident insurance, heavily revised by the Senate to make it non-compulsory for employers, finally became law (1898) and a law on rural credit facilities was passed to secure the support of the peasantry.

Meanwhile the Catholic Church was also responding to the social question. The alienation of the working classes from the Church was seen as a fundamental cause of the Paris Commune and the development of socialism, and some attempts were made in the 1870s to win back the working classes for the faith. Albert de Mun, inspired by the medieval gild system, founded Catholic workers' circles among the artisan élite, while Léon Harmel, whom he met on a pilgrimage in 1873, built a bridge to the industrial working class by bringing crucifixes, chaplains and nuns into his woollen-spinning factory at Val-de-Bois, near Reims. His Confraternity of Our Lady of the Factory, established among his workers in 1875, was copied in a Roubaix linen mill in 1887 by Camille Féron-Vrau, one of the pillars of the Catholic Association of Employers in the Nord, and soon involved 4,000 workers from fifty factories [128].

Catholic reformers were greatly inspired by Pope Leo XIII's encyclical, *Rerum novarum*, published in May 1891, which condemned economic exploitation and urged Catholics to become interested in social reform as the best way to preserve the popular influence of the Church. It also, however, divided them between those, commonly called social Catholics, who saw the function of the Catholic mission as shoring up the existing social hierarchy, and wanted no tampering with it, and those, called Christian democrats, who saw that the only way to make the Church popular again was to divorce it from political reaction and the existing social hierarchy. In the 1890s a wave of *abbés démocrates* therefore committed themselves to the real needs of the working classes and peasantry, campaigning for co-operatives, rural credit institutions and even separate unions for workers and peasants which (to the chagrin of social Catholics) accepted the principle of class struggle. They accepted the Republic, but also championed the intense Catholicism and regionalism of areas like Flanders and Brittany. Thus the abbé Lemire, a seminary teacher, was elected against one royalist noble in Flanders in 1893, and the abbé Gayraud against another in Brittany in 1897 [129; 130]. This electoralism was condemned by the Pope, while bishops were angered by congresses held by *abbé démocrates* up and down the country, which were considered to offer a challenge to the ecclesiastical hierarchy [131; 132]. Despite these obstacles, Christian democracy offered a rare hope of reconciling the Republic and Catholicism, worker and employer, region and nation.

THE RESTORATION OF FRENCH GREATNESS

The Republic as a regime at home was much more contested than the Republic as a power abroad. There were Catholics who believed that the conversion of Clovis on the battlefield of Tolbiac gave France her identity as 'the eldest daughter of the Church', and that Catholics should regard Rome as their fatherland as much as France. But France as a colonial power, establishing hegemony over Muslims, Buddhists and animists, was a Christian and Catholic power, engaged in a civilizing mission. The Republic and the Church went hand in hand. In Gambetta's famous phrase, anti-clericalism was not for export. One of the most influential figures in France's colonial expansion was indeed Lavigerie, the Archbishop of Algiers, capital of her oldest colony. His appointment as papal administrator of Carthage and Tunis in 1881, which gave him jurisdiction over the Italian clergy there, was crucial in France's establishment of a protectorate in Tunis in defiance of Italian claims. As papal delegate for the Sahara and Sudan he sent out his missionaries, the White Fathers, to create new sees in Equatorial Africa and lay the foundations of French power. It is no accident that he was chosen in 1890 to urge French Catholics to accept the Republic whose interests he had done so much to further [133].

A second factor which induced many conservatives to look favourably on the Republic was the Franco-Russian alliance, sealed by military and diplomatic conventions in 1891 and 1892. Under these, Russia agreed to support France if she were attacked by Germany; on the other hand, France was not bound to support Russia in the Dardanelles in any conflict Russia had with Great Britain (which would have been rather different from the Crimean War). The Republic felt secure for the first time in a generation: its isolation, both diplomatic and constitutional, in a Europe of monarchies, was ended. This was symbolized by the visit of a French naval squadron to the Russian base of Kronstadt in July 1891, when the arch-reactionary Tsar, Alexander III, stood bareheaded to a rendering of the *Marseillaise*. The alliance was reinforced by the visit of Tsar Nicholas II and the Tsarina Alexandra to France in October 1896 and the return visit of President Faure to Russia a year later. These were some of the earliest public events caught on film, and the success of them was so great that for a time Méline considered the step (unprecedented since 1877) of holding elections before the Chamber had run its full term.

Rivalry with Great Britain in the colonial sphere was a third factor which induced loyalty to the Republic [134]. Relations had been bad since Anglo-French condominion in Egypt had given way to British military occupation in 1882. An agreement of August 1890 settling a number of African questions was widely considered to be to France's disadvantage. To protest against this and to pursue the goal of French greatness in Africa, a Committee of French Africa was set up. It was headed by the Prince d'Arenberg, the president of the Suez Canal company. Since d'Arenberg was a member of Piou's Constitutional Right and the Committee also included republicans, there was evidence of all-party collaboration on a colonial issue. This was deepened with the formation of an all-party Colonial Group in the Chamber which numbered 90 deputies before the elections of 1893 and 120 afterwards. It was formed mainly of moderates from the republican and conservative sides, and had the active support of Eugène Étienne, the republican deputy for Oran and Under-Secretary of State for Colonies [135]. These pressure groups sharpened their teeth on colonial conflicts with Great Britain. In 1896 the French army put down a revolt in the protectorate of Madagascar and turned it into a colony, but the British had long been influential with the native ruling house, especially through Methodist missionaries, and were accused of fomenting the rebellion. This provoked much popular anti-British and anti-Protestant feeling in France. The long-term plan of the Committee of French Africa was to cut the route Great Britain seemed to be making from the Cape to Cairo by seizing control of the Upper Nile and trying to displace her from Egypt. To this effect an expedition left France in June 1896 under Captain Jean-Baptiste Marchand. As things turned out, however, it was to contribute little to French greatness and something, indirectly, to French domestic instability [136; 137].

7   THE DREYFUS AFFAIR

That the court martial of a Jewish army officer could churn French
life into a foam of passion for the best part of five years and in
some way generate the currents that would inform all French
politics and intellectual controversy in the twentieth century is one
of the paradoxes of the Third Republic [138; 139; 140]. Part of the
explanation lies in France's continuing sense of insecurity and her
eagerness to find scapegoats for her military setbacks. Part of it is to
be found in an eruption of anti-Semitism at the end of the
nineteenth century, less virulent than the strains found in Germany,
Austria and Russia, but remarkable in a country which had a
population of only 80,000 Jews, 0.2 per cent of the total
population. This irrational feeling provoked the intervention of
intellectuals, who believed that the Jewish captain had been
condemned either unjustly or irregularly; in fact the Affair was one
of intellectuals – writers, teachers, students and journalists – far
more than it was one of politicians. In opposition to these
intellectuals there sprang up a new Right which was characterized
less by royalism (though royalism was far from dead) than by a
nationalism that saw France being torn apart by non-French
elements. After the interlude of the 1890s, when some
rapprochement between republicans and conservatives had at least
been attempted, the Dreyfus Affair scored even more deeply the line
dividing republicans from non-republicans. This was because the
'non-French' elements attacked by the nationalists were none other
than the republicans who had run France for the last twenty years,
while the republicans were forced to close ranks to defend the
Republic in danger and their monopoly of political power.

ANTI-SEMITISM

'The anti-Semites do not know the Jews,' wrote Charles Péguy in
1910; 'they talk about them, but they do not know them at all'

[141 *pp. 213–14*]. French Jews were the first in Europe to be emancipated – made citizens – in 1791, and (with the exception of some Yiddish-speaking working-class Jews who had fled from the Russian Empire after 1881) were totally assimilated into the French language, civilization and society. They were *embourgeoisés*, whether in banking, commerce and industry or in the professions, academia and administration [142]. There were 300 Jewish army officers, including Alfred Dreyfus, who was promoted in 1892 to the General Staff. Dreyfus, an Alsatian Jew educated in Paris after Alsace was lost to the Germans, felt no contradiction between his Jewish faith and French citizenship and patriotism [143]. The anti-Semitic press, led by the Assumptionists' *La Croix* and Drumont's *La Libre Parole*, thought otherwise. They played on ancient stereotypes of the Jew as a usurer, cunning schemer, Judas and killer of Christ. They identified Judaism with international capitalism (the Rothschilds) and international socialism (Karl Marx). They argued that Jewish money-power, through ownership of the press and bribery of politicians (the Panama Scandal) controlled the Third Republic. Laws sponsored by Jews liberalizing divorce and founding state secondary schools for girls were denounced as attacks on the Christian family. Lastly, Jews were seen to be the agents of an international Jewish conspiracy to betray France: when military secrets were found in the waste bin of the German military attaché in Paris in 1894 the brilliant young Staff officer, Alfred Dreyfus, was arrested, court-martialled, ritually degraded and sent for life to Devil's Island [144; 145].

There was, however, a small knot of faithful who believed that Dreyfus had not betrayed France and had indeed been framed by certain officers of the general staff. Lieutenant-Colonel Picquart, who took over the Intelligence Section in 1895 and began to suspect irregularities, was hurried off to Tunisia by his superiors. At the end of 1896 the Jewish anarchist, Bernard Lazare, published in Brussels a pamphlet entitled, *A Judicial Error: the Truth about the Dreyfus Affair*. Jews such as Bernard Lazare, Dreyfus's brother Matthieu, and Joseph Reinach (the nephew and son-in-law of Jacques) were at the forefront of the campaign to reopen the case, and were easily denounced as agents of an international Jewish 'syndicate' which intended to discredit the army and ruin France. But they were involved as individuals. The Jews as a community showed no solidarity with Dreyfus; rather they kept their heads down, hoping that the problem would go away [146; 147].

INTELLECTUALS

If the Jewish Dreyfusards belonged to a group, it was to the intellectuals. It was the intellectuals who *created* the Affair [148; 149; 150]. First, they revolutionized the presentation of what was happening. They believed that such fetishisms as the honour of the army, *raison d'Etat*, and racism lay behind the condemnation of Dreyfus and its popular acceptance. They were convinced equally that a scientific examination of the facts would reveal the innocence of Dreyfus and the pernicious role of highly-placed officers, even the former Minister of War, General Mercier [*Doc. 11*]. The acquittal by the military of the man they suspected, Major Esterhazy, in January 1898, acted as a starting-gun for them. Second, the intellectuals were conscious of belonging to a very small group. They were defined as intellectuals against manual workers and politicians and also against the mass of the population, which was seduced by appearances and motivated by prejudice rather than reason. The intellectuals were isolated and persecuted, but drew strength from *camaraderie* and commitment to the cause.

Émile Zola was not the first to make his mark, but his open letter to the President of the Republic under the headline *J'accuse*, published in Clemenceau's paper *L'Aurore* on 13 January 1898, transformed the Affair [*Doc. 12*]. He projected a technical wrangle about evidence as a drama pitting a single individual against the military establishment, Good against Evil, Light against Darkness. 'Poets', he said, 'are in some way visionaries.' He wanted to join the band which was assembling from the four corners of the horizon at 'the crossroads of truth'. His was a mission to unmask the monsters who had sent Dreyfus to Devil's Island, and his letter was 'a revolutionary means to hasten the explosion of truth and justice'. Zola's attack on named army officers was interpreted as libel. He was sent for trial, fined 3,000 francs and sentenced to a year's imprisonment. He fled to London, a martyr to the cause. 'Whoever suffers for truth and justice,' he consoled himself, 'becomes august and sacred' [151 *pp. 19, 93, 104, 126*].

The day after Zola's *J'accuse*, there appeared in the press a *Manifesto of the Intellectuals*. Its signatories included the young writer Marcel Proust and the more established Anatole France, who was a member of the Académie Française. France was writing a series of pieces in the *Écho de Paris* which exposed with the sharp knife of irony the hollowness and hypocrisy of the generals, clergy, nobles and converted Jews who denounced Jewish conspiracy, but he was more sceptical than Zola about the inevitable triumph of justice and truth. 'Peoples, sir,' says one of his characters, 'live on mythology' [152 *p. 199*]. The intellectuals took up their positions at various vantage points. One of these was the offices of the literary and artistic *Revue blanche*. Another was the Bellais bookshop, set up in the Latin Quarter by a graduate of the *École Normale Supérieure*, Charles Péguy. Attacked in the press of his native Orléans for his Dreyfusism and socialism, Péguy declared that 'socialism is the recovery of universal justice, while Dreyfusism is the recovery of a particular justice' [153 *p. 5*]. The librarian of the *École Normale Supérieure*, Lucien Herr, was a man of great conviction who recruited many young Normaliens to the cause [154]. Some, like Blum and Péguy, were also inspired by his socialism. The *École* was more Dreyfusard than socialist, but even as such it was far from being representative of students as a whole. Zola's letter to French youth of December 1897 indeed reproached it for being nationalist and anti-Semitic. Students committed to reopening the Dreyfus case could expect to be beaten up for their pains. The League of Rights of Man, set up during Zola's trial in February 1898 to defend individual rights against militarism, clericalism and nationalism, was another meeting-point of Dreyfusard intellectuals. It included Jews, Protestants, Freemasons and (at first) the liberal Catholic Paul Viollet. However, it remained rather a small organization until the summer of 1898 [155].

POLITICIANS

Politicians reacted in a very different way from intellectuals. They could not deal with truth and falsehood in an abstract sense but had to take public opinion into account. In particular they wanted to be sure of their re-election to parliament, and elections were due in May 1898. Anti-Semitism was a force which any politician ignored at his peril [156]. Zola's trial was greeted by anti-Semitic riots in eastern France (where there were some Jews) and in western France (where there were none). In Algeria, which had a Jewish population of 30,000, there were pogroms. The French Anti-Semitic League was revived in 1897 by a bankrupt oil-refiner, Jules Guérin, with publicity provided by *La Libre Parole*, and campaigned to get Drumont elected at Algiers. Drumont was successful, as were twenty-one other professed anti-Semites, in the elections of 1898 [119; 120]. An analysis of the press in the run-up to the elections shows that only seven of the fifty-five major dailies, six of them

Parisian, were Dreyfusard [157]. Clemenceau, editor of *L'Aurore*, was behaving more like an intellectual than a politician. He had lost his seat as a result of the Panama scandal and was happy in his old role of savaging parliament and ministers. Most of the press either argued that the interests of order, the country and the army had to be put before the interest of an individual, or was blatantly anti-Dreyfusard and anti-Semitic.

It was not that the Left was for Dreyfus and the Right against. There was a plebeian, anticapitalist, left-wing anti-Semitism which the socialist leaders had to confront. Only the anarchists and Allemanists, including Pelloutier and Péguy, were resolutely 'Dreyfusards of the first hour'. This derived from their moralism and their fierce antimilitarism and anticlericalism, but also from the fact that as anarchists they were not seeking election to parliament. Parliamentary socialist leaders were much more prudent. Millerand was deaf to the blandishments of Péguy. Guesde said that Zola's letter was the greatest revolutionary act of the century, but refused to let the working class become involved in a bourgeois civil war which obscured their ultimate goal of collectivism. Jaurès was torn between his intellectual background as a Normalien and academic and his commitment to the masses, which caused him to suspect the Opportunists and Panamists among the Dreyfusards, and to put the unity of the socialist movement before all else. Those who hesitated were lost. Both Jaurès and Guesde lost their seats in the elections of May 1898. Only after the elections did the political landscape change. Jaurès in the wilderness tried to unite the socialists behind the Dreyfusard cause. His perspective on the Affair was now purely Jacobin. 'Since Reaction has formed a bloc' he told a rally in June, 'the Revolution must form a bloc' [100 *p. 237*]. However Guesde feared that Jaurès would run off with the socialist party and refused to follow. The proletariat, he announced, would not tie itself to the tail of 'the bourgeoisie of the prisons and firing squads of 1871' [158 *p. 31*]. It was not until the government sent in 60,000 troops to break a railwaymen's strike in October 1898 that Guesde agreed to align his party with Jaurès and the Dreyfusard front. For a brief moment an alliance of workers and intellectuals had been achieved.

The radicals hated Jules Méline who had displaced them in 1896 and who denied that there was a Dreyfus Affair. But they did not for all that take up the cause of Dreyfus, either before or after the elections of May 1898, which returned them to power. They were much happier attacking the Church than the army. Godefroy Cavaignac, the War Minister in the radical cabinet of Henri Brisson, went so far as to stand up in the Chamber on 9 July 1898 to say that he had irrefutable proof of the guilt of Dreyfus. Jaurès, in an article he published the following month, demonstrated that this 'proof' was a fake produced by an officer in the Intelligence Section, Colonel Henry. Henry confessed to Cavaignac, was duly arrested and slit his throat in prison. More inclined to sympathy with Dreyfus were the moderate republicans, those in the Senate even more than those in the Chamber. The vice-president of the Senate, Auguste Scheurer-Kestner, a Protestant from Alsace, was one of the first and most influential Dreyfusards. Other Protestants and freemasons followed his lead. Many moderates were best described as revisionists: they were persuaded less of Dreyfus's innocence than of the irregularities of military justice in the matter, and therefore pressed for the case to be reopened. Perhaps, as Ferry had said, the Senate was the fortress of the Republic.

NATIONALISM

The suicide of Colonel Henry acted as a catalyst. For the Dreyfusards the military had condemned itself by its own hand and the case for revision was unanswerable. But when certain members of the government, such as the Foreign Minister, Delcassé, began to admit the case for revision, the anti-Dreyfusards hit back, whipping up nationalist sentiment. Domestic politics and foreign affairs became inseparable. Cavaignac and the War Minister who followed him resigned rather than be a party to revision. The government was attacked by the nationalists not only for wavering over Dreyfus, but also for failing to stand up to the British. For at that moment Kitchener, having made his way up the Nile, arrived with far superior numbers at Fashoda, where Captain Marchand had established his base. Delcassé, who was concerned about a possible confrontation with the British navy, wanted a negotiated peace, and offered to recall Marchand. This was discovered by the nationalist press, and a massive demonstration in protest on 28 October 1898 overturned the Brisson government. Delcassé, however, remained Foreign Minister in the next (Dupuy) government which, in the face of the mobilization of the British navy in the Mediterranean, recalled Marchand [159].

The nationalist press was reluctant to see the débâcle in terms of military power. Marchand told it that he had obeyed the order to withdraw after Kitchener had sent him a bundle of French newspapers which related the course of the Affair. He said that he was not inclined to defend a putrid France which, by reopening the Dreyfus case, demonstrated its preference for Jewish traitors over and above the honour of the army. This gave fuel to the opponents of the parliamentary Republic who could argue that it was run by the enemy within who betrayed it to the enemy without [*Doc. 13*]. The nationalist opposition was composed of diverse elements. First there were the royalists who detested the strategy of *Ralliement* which required them either to vote for moderate republicans or to abstain. They wanted to return to intransigence, have done with parliamentary compromise, and mobilize popular support. The *Jeunesses Royalistes* were at the forefront of this movement, but it had the support of the pretender, the Duc d'Orléans, who tried to acquire a popular arm by subsidizing Jules Guérin's Anti-Semitic League and was introduced to the flower of its street-fighters, the butchers of La Villette [160]. A second element was the *Ligue des Patriotes*, which was revived at the end of 1898 by Paul Déroulède [40]. Déroulède was a staunch republican who aspired to a plebiscitary Republic which would be responsive to the popular will. On the other hand there was a strong Bonapartist instinct among the former NCOs and petty bourgeois who made up the League, together with an amenability to the anti-Semitism of Guérin. A third element was the *Ligue de la Patrie Française*. This was founded in January 1899 by some second-rate schoolmasters who then brought in mandarins of the Académie Française such as François Coppée and Jules Lemaître to prove that the Dreyfusards did not have a monopoly of intellectuals. However, its somewhat patrician air and rather woolly philosophy of nationalism (Barrès delivered a lecture to it on *La Terre et les Morts* soon after its foundation) was little to the taste of younger men of extremism and action. These broke away around their own review, the *Action Française*, in July 1899 and planned to raise support in the streets [161].

What the nationalists had in common was their passionate opposition to the revision of the Dreyfus verdict. The 'republican aristocracy' of the Senate were, however, moving in this direction. On the death of President Félix Faure the Senate helped to elect Émile Loubet, who was understood to favour revision. Déroulède decided to pre-empt the issue by staging a *coup d'état* at the funeral of President Faure on 23 February 1899. He grasped the bridle of the horse of one of the generals and tried to persuade him to occupy the Elysée Palace – without success. Déroulède later complained that the royalists had refused their co-operation because of his declared republicanism. The final decision about whether the Dreyfus case should be sent back to the military court lay with the Appeal Court. On 3 June 1899 the Appeal Court ruled that it should. The next day, at the racecourse of Auteuil, President Loubet was set upon by nationalist demonstrators and had his hat knocked off. The cry went up that the Republic was in danger.

FROM *MYSTIQUE* TO *POLITIQUE*

A ministry of republican defence came into office on 22 June under the presidency of René Waldeck-Rousseau. It looked like a classic Jacobin alliance, stretching from moderate republicans through radicals to socialists. On closer inspection it was slightly less convincing. Waldeck was a Progressist, but the Progressists split in two, between a minority which endorsed Waldeck's government, and a majority, led by Méline, which opposed it precisely on the grounds that it was a coalition with radicals and socialists. 'The cabinet included only one radical; the slogan of republican defence was used by Brisson to mobilize reluctant radical support for the ministry. The socialist Millerand was given the Ministry of Commerce, but this did not elicit the support of Guesde, Vaillant and their followers. These marked their distance by shouting 'Vive la Commune', when the new War Minister, General Gallifet, who had helped to suppress it, took his seat in the Chamber, and by announcing on 14 July that they were returning to 'the class and therefore revolutionary policy of the militant proletariat and socialist party' [85 *pp. 423–4*].

The Waldeck-Rousseau ministry presided over the liquidation of the Affair. The second court-martial of Dreyfus opened at Rennes, under the eyes of the nation, in August 1899. An acquittal would have been dangerous, given the state of agitation among the nationalists. An acquittal also ran the risk that members of the general staff and the former War Minister, General Mercier, might be threatened with trial, and be tempted to launch a *coup d'etat* [162]. However, on 9 September Dreyfus was once more found guilty by a majority of the judges, albeit with the ridiculous qualification of 'extenuating circumstances'. Ten days later Dreyfus received a pardon from the President of the Republic. This was probably the most politic outcome for which Waldeck could have wished. But the Dreyfusards were infuriated. The clear acquittal which would have resolved the struggle between Good and Evil, Light and Darkness, was not offered to them. Their anger was deflected by the government on to the extreme nationalists,

Déroulède and Guérin, who were made into examples (accused of plotting against state security, taken before the High Court, smeared with royalist connections and sentenced respectively to six years' exile and ten years' imprisonment) and on to the Catholic Church, in particular the Assumptionists who published the anti-Semitic *La Croix* and were dissolved. By contrast, the military men under suspicion were amnestied. As Zola put it, the virtuous and the rascals were put into the same bag.

The liquidation of the Affair revealed a shift between what Péguy called *mystique* and *politique*. The sense of mission of the first Dreyfusards gave way to the calculations of parties and the accommodation of interests. Dreyfusism became part of republican legitimacy, although as Péguy pointed out, those who laid claim to the mantle of Dreyfus in 1903 were just as likely to have been anti-Dreyfusard in 1898. When Péguy espoused Catholicism in 1910 with his *Mystery of the Charity of Joan of Arc*, the Catholic conservatives toasted his conversion to the Right. But, he insisted in *Notre Jeunesse*, published a few months later, Catholicism as a religion had nothing to do with Catholicism as a political position. At the beginning of the Affair, he argued, it had been possible, at the level of *mystique*, to be republican and Christian and even Jewish at the same time, for what had Dreyfusism been if not 'a religion of temporal salvation' [141 *p. 242*]? A 'Republic of Dreyfusards' was now in power, but it represented the revenge of the politicians who had never demonstrated any of the generous commitment of the Dreyfusards of the first hour. They politicized the Affair and turned its cause into a familiar intolerant anticlericalism.

8   RADICALISM

Radicalism was at once the most characteristic political force in France between 1898 and 1914 and the most difficult to define. A book published by Madeleine Rebérioux in 1975 is entitled *La République radicale?*, complete with question mark [3]. This is not unreasonable. It is open to debate whether the Radicals held power in this period, whether they constituted a proper political party and whether their policies were indeed radical.

If we look at personalities it is possible to distinguish 'old' radicals and 'new' radicals. Some radicals of a chauvinist bent, like Déroulède and Rochefort, moved across the political spectrum to the nationalist Right; what remained constant was their hatred of parliamentary oligarchy. Others, like Millerand and Jaurès, who wished for a more 'social' Republic, moved in the direction of socialism. Radicals who achieved power before the Boulanger Affair, including Floquet and Goblet, were phased out by the Panama scandal and the passage of time. The 'new' radicals came to prominence in the wake of Panama, and included Bourgeois and Brisson, who became prime ministers respectively in 1895 and 1898. They might be described as more calculating and less passionate, more realistic and less romantic. Clemenceau is not easy to classify. His career spans the whole Third Republic but it was interrupted by Panama and did not really bear fruit again until 1906, when he formed a government. Moreover, though he was in the popular view the quintessential radical, he was not a member of the Radical party except in the year 1909.

This introduces a second distinction, between radicalism as a movement and the Radical party. In a country where universal suffrage was so long established, it is perhaps surprising that organized mass parties took so long to evolve. It took the Dreyfus Affair, and the consequent agitation of opinion and raising of stakes, to provoke the organization of parties with a recognizable discipline and ideology. The need for definition either within or against the Waldeck coalition and the approaching elections of 1902 had a galvanizing effect. Among the radicals the initiative came less from the parliamentary politicians than from the constituents. A congress held in June 1901 brought together in Paris representatives from hundreds of masonic lodges, secularist societies, provincial newspapers, local committees and municipalities as well as deputies and senators. The local Committees were organized in the countryside by small proprietors, in the towns by artisans, shopkeepers and public employees, while the party leadership and deputies were lawyers, doctors, teachers, journalists and businessmen. The wide spectrum of opinion in the party was clear in its title, the 'Republican, Radical and Radical-Socialist Party' [163; 164; 165; 166].

Other groups of politicians saw the need to follow suit. In the same month former *Ralliés* around Albert de Mun and Jacques Piou set up a Liberal Action party, which hoped to build bridges towards non-Radical republicans [167]. These fell into two groups, which came to call themselves parties, but lacked any real constituency organization. The first, launched in October 1901, was the Democratic Alliance, composed of pro-Waldeck Progressists who were against socialism but for reform, anticlerical but not antireligious. Representing the universities, magistracy and administration, close to financial and colonial interests, it included Louis Barthou, Raymond Poincaré, Maurice Rouvier, Eugène Étienne and Joseph Caillaux [168]. The second, formed in 1903, was the Republican Federation, composed of Progressists who had broken with Waldeck and his coalition, were hostile to radicalism as well as to socialism and supported Catholicism. Representing landowners and big business it included Jules Méline and Eugène Motte, the textile magnate of Roubaix who had defeated Guesde in 1898.

The socialists had been the first to set up party organizations, but it still proved impossible to hold together a single socialist party. The inclusion of a socialist minister, Millerand, in the ministerial coalition provoked a crisis at the first congress of socialist organizations held in Paris in December 1899 to establish a French Socialist Party. Jaurès defended ministerial participation as the natural consequence of participation in municipalities and parliament. But this was rejected by Guesde who argued that Millerand was a hostage of the bourgeoisie and that ministerial participation only divided and emasculated the socialists, who instead should remain united behind the banner of class war. At the second congress in September 1900 the split was wide open. Guesde formed his own Socialist Party of France, while Jaurès called imminent social revolution a hallucination. In a democracy, he said, power must be won legally by a majority, not by a revolutionary minority. The Republic was not necessarily bourgeois; it was an instrument of social justice and the 'political form of socialism'. He summed up, 'the Republic is incomplete without socialism, but socialism is powerless without the Republic' [169 *p. 141*].

The Radicals, like the followers of Jaurès, were tied into the Waldeck-Rousseau coalition by the ideology of republican defence. They were militant defenders of the Republic against threats from Church and army manifested during the Dreyfus Affair. They welcomed 'all the sons of the Revolution, whatever their differences, against all the partisans of counter-revolution' [163 *p. 124*]. They were opposed to large-scale monopoly capitalism in the name of the small businesses run by so many of their supporters. On the other hand they opposed socialist plans to collectivize property (with the possible exception of mines, railways and utilities), believing that workers should gain access to private property, the condition of individual liberty, by hard work, education, setting up their own businesses, or participating in co-operatives or profit-sharing schemes. They preferred the fusion of classes to class struggle, believed that the better-off should contribute something to the welfare of children, women, the old and the sick, and in particular demanded old-age pensions for retired workers to be funded out of progressive income tax [*Doc. 14a*] [170; 171].

Some measures of social reform were passed under the Waldeck-Rousseau ministry. The Radical navy minister Camille Pelletan, recognized unions set up by civilian naval personnel and agreed an eight-hour day in naval workshops. Millerand as Minister of Commerce extended the ten-hour limit on the working day imposed on female workshops (1892) to mixed workshops (1900), and saw through an Associations law which enabled trade unions to hold property collectively (July 1901). Joseph Caillaux, the son of a minister who had held office as a result of the 16 May *coup* and anxious to establish his republican credentials as a young Finance Minister, introduced the progressive principle in his reform of death duties. On the other hand Millerand's plan for the compulsory arbitration of industrial disputes was opposed both by employers and trade unions and failed, while no progress was made on pensions or progressive income tax [172]. Several factors account for this. First, the Radical party had a left wing and a right wing, and the parliamentarians were generally more cautious than local militants. Second, the Waldeck-Rousseau ministry was a coalition of different interests, including the Democratic Alliance which had business concerns at heart. Third, the main agenda of the government – and the one issue on which it could agree – was the defence of the Republic. Defence against a *coup d'état* was undertaken in secret by police surveillance of Catholic, reactionary army officers [173]. Defence against the Church's interference in politics was undertaken publicly by the dissolution, under the Associations law, of religious congregations which had not applied for, or received, proper authorization under Napoleonic legislation. As a Breton, Waldeck understood that Catholicism and republicanism were entirely compatible, and proposed that religious congregations dissolved in one location might be allowed to continue in another, depending on the view expressed by municipal councils. His was an anticlericalism in search of consensus [31].

THE *BLOC DES GAUCHES*

In April–May 1902 the Waldeck-Rousseau government was victorious in the parliamentary elections. The Right with 264 seats, was confined to the North, North-East and West. On the government side, however, (321 seats) there was a marked shift from moderates to Radicals, which provoked the resignation of Waldeck from the premiership. The Radicals had lost Paris to the Right in 1900, but were now as strong in the countryside as in the towns, calling themselves simply 'radical' in the North of France, and 'radical-socialist' in the South. Among the socialists the supporters of Jaurès and republican defence did much better than Guesde and the revolutionaries.

Waldeck was succeeded as premier by Émile Combes, a country doctor from the South-West, the Radical leader in the Senate. He headed a coalition called the *Bloc des Gauches*, which was steered by a committee including Jaurès and had an ample social programme, but which also had to accommodate moderates like the banker Maurice Rouvier, and therefore dedicated itself to anti-clericalism [174; 175]. This was tactically rational, but it would be unwise to underestimate the force of anticlericalism as a political passion, either in the case of Combes, who had once taught in the Assumptionist College of Nîmes, or in that of the Radical grassroots. They wanted to destroy the influence of the Catholic

Church in politics and education once and for all. Combes used his majority to dissolve the religious congregations wholesale, rejecting their petitions for authorization *en bloc* and taking no account of local feeling. Much local feeling was passionately committed to the congregations, especially to nuns, who were often recruited locally and provided for education and welfare in the community. This was the case not only in royalist areas but also in areas, like the tip of Brittany, which were otherwise decidedly republican [130]. *Gendarmes* and even troops had to be sent in to expel the nuns, who were protected by demonstrators barricading themselves into schoolhouses. Albert de Mun tried to channel this groundswell of Catholic opinion by refounding his party as the Popular Liberal Action. More serious were the cracks which appeared in the *Bloc des Gauches*. Waldeck-Rousseau did not approve of the dissolution of overseas missions and female teaching congregations and made things very difficult for Combes in the Senate.

At the other end of the coalition, socialist leaders were worried that the anticlerical crusade was weakening their grip on the working class. However, the sharpening of class conflict was beginning to reveal the true colours of the ruling Radical party. When a general miners' strike threatened in October 1902, Combes sent in the military and one miner was killed in the Loire. Anarchists like Pouget and Blanquists like the shoemaker Griffuelhes rose to power in the CGT, making possible the union of the CGT and the Federation of *Bourses du Travail* in 1902 and the defeat of moderate unions led by the printers at the Bourges congress of the CGT in September 1904. From now on the CGT was committed to a general strike for an eight-hour day, which was seen by the militants as a consciousness-raiser for a revolutionary general strike. Socialist leaders moved with the current, willingly or unwillingly. Millerand interpellated the Combes ministry in March 1904 for ignoring social reform [*Doc. 14b*]. At the Amsterdam meeting of the Socialist International in August 1904, Jaurès was defeated by motions sponsored by the German Social Democrats in favour of revolutionary action and the class struggle. As a result he had to leave the *Bloc des Gauches* and defer to Guesde in a united socialist party, the French Section of the Workers' International (SFIO). The Combes ministry was finally discredited by the *affaire des fiches*, in which use of Freemasons to keep tabs on reactionary army officers and to promote republican ones was exposed, and was replaced in November 1904 by a cabinet led by Maurice Rouvier.

One last anticlerical card was played in an attempt to keep the socialists in line. The socialists had long wanted the Separation of Church and State – the termination of government subsidies to the Church and, in turn, of government powers, including the appointment of bishops. Combes had refused to countenance any relaxation of government control over the Church, but the price of socialist support was now Separation, and this was seen through by Aristide Briand, who chaired the parliamentary commission on the Separation. The bill was passed in December 1905 and Catholic opposition brushed aside. But that did not mean that the socialists were happy. For social strife was now reaching a pitch that the clarion calls of anticlericalism could not hope to drown.

CLASS WAR

1906 was the worst year for strikes before 1936, which in turn was the worst before 1968 [66; 176]. They were spontaneous and violent, in response to the rising cost of living and at the fringe of a wave of strikes whose epicentre was Russia. Following the pit disaster at Courrières in the Pas-de-Calais in which 1,100 miners died, a CGT-affiliated 'young' union broke away from the 'old' union of the miners' deputy, Basly, and brought 40,000 men out on strike. The government replied by pouring 20,000 troops into the northern coalfield [177]. At Hennebont in Brittany metallurgical workers who went on strike for 116 days in the spring and summer of 1906 were reduced to eating crabs from the beach. The CGT launched a general strike for an eight-hour day on 1 May 1906. This was opposed by the Guesdists, who, though revolutionary, wanted workers to defer to the leadership of the party and confine themselves to voting in the elections of 6 May. But 200,000 workers responded to the strike call. In Paris many of the bourgeoisie feared another Commune and started to leave. Clemenceau, then Minister of the Interior, declared a state of siege, sent in troops and arrested CGT leaders, declaring, 'Your means of action is disorder, my duty is to ensure order' [178 *p. 210*].

In October 1906 Clemenceau became premier. He included in his cabinet two former socialists, Briand and Viviani – the latter at a newly-created Ministry of Labour – but also moderates like Caillaux and Barthou. There was no sign that class conflict was easing. The CGT met in congress at Amiens that same month and formally affirmed the independence of the trade-union movement. The Charter of Amiens, which came to acquire mythical status in the labour movement, asserted that while individual trade-unionists were free to vote in elections, the trade-union movement as such declared itself independent of political parties, not least the SFIO. Strife continued for another two years. Sectors and regions not previously involved in strikes and unionization were mobilised. In the recently mechanized boot and shoe industry there was a strike of 103 days at Fougères in Brittany in the winter of 1906–7 and another at Raon l'Etape in the Vosges, where two workers were killed. Primary school teachers formed unions after 1904, gathered in a national federation in 1905 and demanded the right to affiliate to *Bourses du Travail* and the CGT. This was refused by the government in 1907 and recalcitrant teachers were dismissed. Along the Mediterranean coast winegrowers rose in revolt in the summer of 1907 against the government's failure to regulate overproduction and fraud. Troops fired on demonstrators at Narbonne and Montpellier, but at Béziers they refused to fire and mutinied [179; 180]. The sand-quarriers of the Seine struck with the help of more skilled building workers in May 1908. The employers brought in blacklegs who were seized by the strikers. The *gendarmes* released the blacklegs, killing two strikers in the process. Tension between the government and the labour movement reached a pitch [*Doc. 15*]. The builders' union, with the support of the CGT, called a one-day protest strike and demonstration on 30 July. This was charged by troops, leaving another two dead. Clemenceau arrested and imprisoned the CGT leaders and would have banned the CGT but for the intervention of Viviani and Briand [181]. A general strike called by the CGT was a failure, and this marked a turning point in the strike movement. Basly's miners' union joined the CGT in June 1908, which reinforced its moderate wing. The revolutionary secretary of the CGT, Griffuelhes, was replaced in 1909 by Léon Jouhaux, while in the SFIO influence was passing from Guesde to Jaurès. Both Jouhaux and Jaurès put organization and unity before ideological purity [182].

RADICALS BETWEEN REVOLUTION AND REVOLUTION

The Radical party was increasingly subjected to tensions which were both ideological and institutional. Ideologically, the separation of Church and State concluded the anticlerical mission on which Radicals had all been able to agree and forced them to re-examine social questions. On the other hand, the outbreak of class war forced them to decide whether their alliance with the socialists was sensible and their commitment to the principles of the French

Revolution anything more than rhetorical. Institutionally, the Radicals constituted the necessary foundation of any ministry and provided a good number of ministers, but as a party they were not in the driving seat. The key figures between 1906 and 1909 were the Prime Minister, Clemenceau, who was a member of the Radical party only in 1909, and Caillaux, the Finance Minister, who did not become a Radical until 1912. Broadly, the right wing of the Radical party was hesitant about Caillaux while the left wing was increasingly hostile to Clemenceau. Caillaux had the reputation of a 'plutocratic demagogue', a man of private means and fine pedigree who was bent on disciplining the very wealthy in the interests of the public good. He had the support of the socialists and radical-socialists, but his policies were too extreme for moderate Radicals. His plan to nationalize the railway companies was pared down until it involved the nationalization of only the bankrupt Western Railway, which Jaurès called 'a rotten egg'. His bill to establish progressive income tax, which was a fundamental reform of France's archaic direct tax system in order to tap the real sources of wealth, was also too much for many Radicals to stomach. The bill passed through the Chamber in March 1909, but Radicals felt secure in the hope that the Senate would oppose it. The bill was sent to a Senate commission chaired by Maurice Rouvier, a known adversary of income tax, where it was lost [172]. A bill on old-age pensions, passed by the Chamber in 1906, was similarly held up.

The left wing of the Radical party now distanced itself from Clemenceau. He guaranteed order, but many considered his tactics unnecessarily brutal and even provocative. Clemenceau did not object to his image as the 'first cop in France', increasingly disassociated himself from his Finance Minister, and curried favour with the Democratic Alliance and the Republican Federation. Disagreement was also intense on the question of whether civil servants had the right to form trade unions and strike. Radical-socialists wanted this right enshrined in law; Clemenceau refused. When postal workers went on strike in March 1909 Clemenceau broke the strike and had 500 of them dismissed for union activism. The executive committee of the Radical party criticized the 'retrograde tendencies' of the government and passed a motion of no confidence. In July 1909 a third of the Radicals voted against him in the Chamber and brought down his ministry. Clemenceau's successor, Briand, also sailed too close to the Right for the taste of Radicals. He was a former socialist now firmly in the moderate camp. In March 1910, with an eye to the elections of

April and May, he and Viviani finally pushed through the pensions law. But when the railway workers went on strike in October, Briand showed his true mettle by drafting the strikers into the army. This authoritarianism, and the electoral success of socialists in the south of France at their expense, drove the Radical congress to accuse Briand of appeasing the Right. Briand was forced to resign and reconstitute his cabinet with more Radicals.

The Radicals prohibited consorting with the Right under the rules of republican legitimacy, but the rule of 'no enemies on the Left' could be difficult to follow. Moderate Radicals saw a solution in electoral reform: if single-member constituencies were replaced by proportional representation, the Radicals would no longer have to make electoral compromises with socialists and, their hands free, would be able to claim the middle ground between the socialists and the Right. However, successive party congresses rejected PR in favour of retaining the single-member constituency. There was a fear that PR would unduly favour the socialists, and even the Right, whereas under the existing system the socialists were required as often as not to stand down for the Radical candidate against the candidate of the Right according to the rules of republican discipline. There was a premium on keeping the formula which had produced Radical France.

Pressure was mounting from another direction to induce the Radicals to change the electoral system. The feminist movement was not only concerned with voting rights: Napoleon's Civil Code, which restricted the rights of women in questions of marriage and property, had long been an object of hatred. In 1904, when the French establishment was celebrating the centenary of the Code, a copy of it was burned in Paris by a group of feminists. In 1907 a law finally gave married French women control of their earnings. Feminists campaigning for the vote were divided between seeking to convert the Radical and socialist parties by persuasion, and direct action. Radicals and socialists supported a bill to give women the vote in local elections, seen as closer to the hearth, in 1906, but it then went to a parliamentary commission chaired by Ferdinand Buisson. Buisson, author of the Radical programme and founder member of the League of Rights of Man, produced a report in favour of women's suffrage in 1909, but women's suffrage was subordinated to resolving the issue of PR. Clemenceau did not even try to seem open-minded. In a pamphlet published in 1907 he rehearsed old fears of the Catholic vote and the danger run by the Republic. 'If the right to vote were given to women tomorrow,' he stated, 'France would all of a sudden jump backwards into the Middle Ages' [184 *p. 99*]. Some feminists, such as the veteran suffragist Hubertine Auclert and the psychiatric doctor Madeleine Pelletier, resorted to direct action, overturning ballot boxes in a Paris polling station during the 1908 municipal elections. Others formed a French Union for Women's Suffrage (UFSF) the same year, to strive for the vote by 'moderate, bourgeois' means, avoiding the 'ridicule' attracted by imitating British suffragettes. Pelletier managed to convert the SFIO formally to support votes for women, but they tended to regard feminism as bourgeois and a distraction from class struggle. Auclert and Pelletier were among a number of women who ran as candidates in the 1910 parliamentary elections, but they were cold-shouldered by the UFSF and Pelletier was given an unwinnable seat by the SFIO [183; 184; 185; 186; 187].

The tension within the Radical party between radicalism and moderation was not resolved until the Radicals were rudely thrust from power. The Prime Minister, Caillaux, was accused of failing to protect France's interests against Germany at the time of the second Morocco crisis at the beginning of 1912 (which will be discussed in Chapter 9) and obliged to resign. The victory was that of the moderates of the Democratic Alliance, with help from the Catholic Right. Poincaré became President of the Council in January 1912, and he won over Albert de Mun and the Catholic Right by relaxing the lay laws, dissolving teachers' unions on the grounds of antipatriotism, and gracing his civil marriage by a church wedding. He was elected President of the Republic with the help of the Right in January 1913. He appointed Briand, then Barthou, premier, and made a bid for nationalist support by strengthening the French army, increasing military service from two years to three [188].

Revenge came swiftly. Caillaux, cast from office, decided that the best way back was through a streamlined Radical party. He won the contest for the leadership at the Pau congress of October 1913, and introduced a programme which would slough off from the party those who were Radical in no more than name and make way for a tactical alliance with the SFIO in the elections of April 1914. The programme revolved round abrogation of the three-year military service law, defence of the lay school, and the establishment of progressive income tax [189]. In December 1913 the new Radical-Socialist party and the SFIO overthrew Barthou, and Caillaux returned as Finance Minister in what was to be a caretaker government until the elections. Barthou and the moderates hired the *Figaro* to discredit Caillaux as a wheeler-dealer who had used ministerial office for private gain. When the press favourable to Caillaux rebutted all these charges, the *Figaro* prepared to expose his private life, notably his affair with his present second wife during his first marriage. Henriette Caillaux stopped the revelations by shooting the editor [190]. The Radical-Socialists and SFIO triumphed in the elections of April 1914 and Caillaux and Jaurès planned the formation of a joint ministry in the autumn. However, by then Caillaux's career, despite the acquittal of his wife, was ruined; Jaurès was dead; and Europe was plunged into war.

9 NATIONALISM

The Third Republic was born out of the defeat of the Second Empire and was itself at once defeated by Prussia. It lived until 1914 under the shadow of defeat, but defeat had to be rationalized in order to make life bearable [191]. 'The Frenchman,' said Trochu, the military governor of Paris during the Franco-Prussian war, 'has a special aptitude for explaining his defeats' [192 p. 23]. Explanations were usually determined by interest or ideology. The republicans blamed ignorance: the French had been taught a lesson by the Prussian schoolmaster. They traced this ignorance to the 'obscurantism' of the Church schools and thus reinforced their argument for diminishing the Church's influence in education. 'We must put the gymnast and the soldier alongside the primary school teacher,' said Gambetta in 1871, to train 'a new generation, strong, intelligent, as enamoured of science as of the fatherland' [193 p. 23].

The Catholic Right interpreted defeat in a completely different way. They blamed the apostasy of the French nation, which in the last century had strayed from the ways of God. Its sins included liberalism, democracy, socialism, science and materialism, and the abandonment in 1870 of the Holy City of Rome which it had protected with its troops from revolution and nationalism since 1849. The scourges of Prussian soldiers (Protestant, materialist) and Communards (atheist, materialist) had been sent by God to chastize France. Only when the French repented and returned to the ways of God would God's grace be forthcoming. These sentiments were behind the subscription to build the basilica of Sacré-Cœur on the top of the Communard stronghold of Montmartre, pilgrimages to the shrines of Lourdes and Paray-le-Monial, and the unveiling of Frémiet's statue of Joan of Arc in Paris in 1875 (194; 195; 196). A third explanation, favoured by the revolutionary Left, blamed the fear of the propertied classes that war, as in 1792, required mass mobilization and that mass mobilization might unleash revolutionary forces [*Doc. 16*]. Paris was already seething when an armistice with Prussia was sought by what Marx ironically called 'the Government of National Defection' [197 *p. 16*]. While Gambetta wanted war to the death with Prussia, involving a *levée en masse*, Thiers and his allies wanted a truce with Prussia in order to bring Paris under control [9]. The Paris Commune was a revolutionary and patriotic response to reactionaries and *capitulards*. In turn, Thiers hurried to finalize peace terms so that French prisoners of war would be free to cross Prussian lines to suppress the Commune [12]. There were few wars fought by France after the Revolution which were not civil wars as well.

REBUILDING NATIONAL CONFIDENCE

France had gone to war in 1870 to defend her leadership of Europe from the challenge of Germany. After the defeat of the Empire, the Republic strove valiantly to lay claim to the greatness it had forfeited, reviving the tradition of the *Grande Nation* which went back to the revolutionary wars of the 1790s. 'Let the lion of 1792 draw itself up and bristle', proclaimed Victor Hugo [198 *p. 139*].

The Republic, like the Empire, was quickly overwhelmed and thinkers like Ernest Renan argued, as Montesquieu had done before, that greatness was impossible in a republic. A number of strategies were adopted, however, to restore the national confidence of the French, and to give the Republic some lustre of greatness. First, it was asserted that though France had lost the war, honour had been saved. The *Chants du Soldat* of the veteran Déroulède and the paintings of Alphonse de Neuville concentrated on isolated acts of heroism of small groups of soldiers in the 1870 war, fighting to the bitter end against overwhelming odds. Second, the pain of the defeat of 1870 was reduced by placing it in the context of French history as a whole, the secular rivalry with the Germans, and the continuity of French greatness. The influential school textbooks of Ernest Lavisse, formerly tutor to the Prince Imperial, charted a long process of nation-building which bound together monarchies and republics, setbacks and triumphs [199]. Third, a new view of nationhood was put forward by Ernest Renan in a Sorbonne lecture given in 1882. He argued that the nation was defined not by race, territory or religion but by a collective memory of fighting together and the collective will to fight together in the future. He believed that collective suffering united more than collective joy and, therefore, that the pain of defeat in 1870 could be put to excellent use in rebuilding national solidarity [*Doc. 17*]. The statue of Strasbourg in the Place de la Concorde draped in black, the schoolmaps of France with Alsace-Lorraine blotted out, Daudet's tear-jerking story, *The Last Lesson*, in which the French teacher, about to cede his class to a German teacher, consoles his pupils, were all designed, paradoxically, to strengthen French national sentiment and collective will.

How to use that collective resolve, however, was a matter that divided the French. Jules Ferry and the Opportunists argued that the only way to recover greatness was by acquiring colonies, which would not antagonize Bismarck and indeed for which Bismarck's help might be elicited [*Doc. 18a*]. For instance, Bismarck helped France gain a protectorate in Tunisia in 1882, if only to frighten Italy (whose interests in Tunisia were overridden) into a Triple Alliance with Germany and Austria-Hungary and presided over the conference in Berlin in 1884–5 which partitioned Africa [200]. On the other hand there were those, such as Déroulède, his *Ligue des Patriotes*, Clemenceau and the radicals, who insisted that France must prepare for *revanche* against Germany to regain Alsace and Lorraine, and must not waste men and resources on colonial adventures in North Africa and Indo-China which would weaken France when war eventually came on the Rhine. Clemenceau waged a successful campaign against Ferry on this score [*Doc. 18b*], although this passionate patriotism was somewhat discredited by association with General Boulanger.

THE ARMY

The army was both the fighting force of the Republic and a political entity. Despite the *coups d'état* of 1799 and 1851 France did not have a tradition of intervention of the military in politics, although the loyalty of the army to the Republic was sometimes open to question. The officer corps was not an aristocratic caste – 38 per cent of divisional generals were noble in 1876–8, 19 per cent in 1901, and the proportion was lower further down the hierarchy. But many officers had served previous regimes, including those imperial officers who had been captured at Metz and Sedan in 1870 and then reintegrated into the army. According to Gambetta's files in 1874–5, 88 per cent of divisional generals were hostile to the Republic [201]. The problem did not diminish with retirements. Those of doubtful loyalty to the Republic were excluded by the republicans from politically sensitive posts in the administration and magistrature and had little choice of career apart from the army. Moreover, the military academy of Saint-Cyr recruited increasingly from Catholic colleges, which educated a social elite ill-disposed to the state *lycées*, forging the alliance, as the epithet had it, of 'the sabre and the holy-water sprinkler' [202 *p. 201;* 173].

The army had a role internally as well as externally, as a guarantor of social order. In some ways it was better at this than at winning battles. The shame of surrender to the Prussians was in part redeemed by the suppression of the Commune. The revolutionary force in Paris, the National Guard, was disbanded in 1871, and the army reform of 1872 deliberately avoided the model of the nation-in-arms, which Thiers described as 'putting a gun on the shoulder of every socialist' [203 *pp. 39–40*]. Military service was made compulsory, but it was not universal or short-term. There were many exemptions and half the contingent did five years' service while the other half, which could not be accommodated, did six months. The aim of the republicans when they came to power was to integrate the army more with the nation, making it less like a standing army [204; 205]. Boulanger as War Minister planned the reduction of military service to three years and claimed, during the miners' strike at Decazeville, that each soldier was sharing his ration of soup with a miner. The *Bloc des Gauches* cut military service again in 1904 to two years. Nevertheless, the inadequacy of the gendarmerie meant that the army was regularly used to control strikes and demonstrations. A bill to form a mobile corps of 2,000 *gendarmes* in April 1906 failed to pass the Chamber; the Left saw it as the instrument of *coups d'état*, while the Right feared it would become a tool of anticlericalism, to clear protesting Catholics from schools and churches. The pugnacious Clemenceau perhaps had no choice but to employ the army against the labour movement in 1906–8, but in no sense did he pull his punches [206].

Anti-militarism and a cult of the army co-existed in the generation before the war. The other ranks had always been brutally treated, but the military service law of 1889 constrained to service many sons of educated middle-class families who would previously have been exempt. The following years saw a rash of anti-military novels which criticized mindless discipline and the privileges of the officer corps [207]. At the same time the military were scoring a number of victories in Indo-China and Africa, such as the conquest of Madagascar in 1896, which fired the popular imagination. The popular press was full of stories and images (some less than authentic) of the atrocities of races and regimes in hotter climates and of the benefits of Western civilization brought by the soldier and the missionary [208]. The Dreyfus Affair was a confrontation of these two perspectives. For some, military justice beyond the purview of the civil courts was the epitome of military privilege and tyranny over individual rights which had been sanctified by the French Revolution. For others, military justice could not be questioned without weakening the army and France itself. These found it difficult to believe that in the same army that took part in manoeuvres and marches with bridles jangling and flags fluttering there were officers who were forging documents in back rooms. The view that a 'syndicate' of Jews and intellectuals were out to rubbish it was easily believed. Now that the monarchy had been abolished, the army – albeit the army of the Republic – was seen to represent the present embodiment of a glorious past which should be set apart and idolized.

NATIONALIST MOVEMENTS

The nationalist movements which emerged at the time of the Dreyfus Affair attacked the supine attitude of the government toward Great Britain. But they were not in favour of war. They were opposed to the republican oligarchy which had monopolized power for twenty years and used the rhetoric of 'the Republic in danger' to keep office within their own magic circle. Every attempt to open the 'closed' Republic, whether by threat or blandishment, had failed. Boulangism and the Panama scandal had not swept the oligarchy away. Those moderates who had bowed to the republican regime had found some sympathy from Méline, but after the elections of 1898 Méline was out of power and the door firmly closed on them by the radicals. The new strategy of the opposition was to attack the republican political class as anti-French or non-French. It was accused of being a minority which did not truly reflect French opinion but which had perfected a machinery for taking and retaining power. It was accused also of peddling foreign ideologies and betraying France's interests to the foreigner. The opposition sought to marginalize the ruling elite and claim for itself a legitimacy based on the representation of French interests and Frenchness.

The identification of the republican oligarchy with the Jews went back to Drumont's *La France juive*. In 1898 and 1899 the smear of Protestantism and Freemasonry was also liberally applied. The Protestants were portrayed as a party which had organized the conquest of power under the Republic, as a community which had been emancipated at the Revolution and turned to persecute the

Catholic Church, and as a fifth column, if not a foreign, Germanic, race, which had served the interests of Prussia and Great Britain since the sixteenth century [209]. The Freemasons were similarly criticized as machine men, the wire-pullers behind the Radical party, as anticlerical, antimilitary and (since they belonged to an international confraternity) as indifferent patriots.

If the republican oligarchy did not fit into any of these categories, then they were associated with the intellectuals and academics who had mounted the Dreyfus Affair. This was the basic theme of the writings of Maurice Barrès. Barrès argued that these 'aristocrats of thought' regarded the masses as stupid and traditional. They wanted to uproot the masses from their past and their backgrounds in order to bring them into the bright light of republican morality and patriotism. The unity of France would be forged in the classroom; France was nothing but 'a set of ideas'. Barrès's view was that intellectuals should grasp the contradiction of trying to convert stupid people to their republican philosophy. In any case, though the masses might be stupid in their terms, there were untold treasures in 'the national unconscious, the sure instinct of the masses' [210 *pp. 267–90*]. That unconscious was determined by forces which preceded and enfolded the individual, the weight of heredity and environment. To try to uproot people from these influences was to defy reality. Instead, those who were looking to restore the 'moral unity' of France should accept these determining forces. Nationalism for Barrès thus became the cult of the forces which had made the French: ancestors and soil. National feeling was created among the crowds who attended the funeral of Victor Hugo in 1885, in those who descended the valley of the Moselle, or in those who visited the war cemeteries of 1870, where French blood and soil were mingled.

Some historians have argued that nationalism switched at the turn of the century from being a doctrine on the Left to being a doctrine on the Right [211]. In fact, the main development was that a patriotism which identified France with the Republic was challenged by a nationalism which disconnected France and the Republic. This nationalism claimed that France's true interests were not represented by the politicians who currently held power in the Republic. That did not mean that they were opposed to the Republic as a regime, but it made possible a rapprochement under the nationalist banner of those who had different views about the regime. For instance, both strict republicans and Bonapartists could agitate in Déroulède's *Ligue des Patriotes*. The *Ligue de la Patrie Française* by and large subscribed to the ideas of Barrès: nationalist without being racist, given the Flemish, Breton and Basque elements in the French nation; and not loyal to a particular dynasty, for the French had lived under monarchies, empires and republics, and were still French. There was one exception to this rule. The *Action Française,* which was born under the wing of the *Ligue de la Patrie Française*, was originally formed of Bonapartists and radicals who had· refused to follow Clemenceau into the Dreyfusard camp, and demanded a strong authoritarian (instead of a parliamentary) Republic. But in 1900 it came under the influence of Charles Maurras, an admirer of Renan, who saw the salvation of France only in the restoration of the monarchy. His argument was not sentimental but, in his view, ruthlessly logical. All the Great European Powers, according to Maurras, were monarchies; France was not great and she was a republic; therefore France could recover greatness only if she restored the monarchy [*Doc. 19*].

TOWARDS THE *UNION SACRÉE*

In 1904 the Entente Cordiale settled the rivalry between France and Great Britain in Africa – France recognized Britain's supremacy in Egypt, while Britain recognized France's interest in Morocco. Now France faced the challenge of German power and pretensions, and her greatness was put squarely to the test. In 1905 Germany took advantage of the defeat of France's ally, Russia, at the hands of the Japanese and the ensuing revolution in Russia to provoke France into war over her Moroccan ambitions. France stood firm, with the support of Great Britain, but from this moment the possibility of war with the old enemy, Germany, was a fact of French life.

The crisis gave a boost to nationalist groups [212]. The *Action Française* launched a daily paper of the same name in 1908, which was hawked about by street runners, the *Camelots du Roy*, who doubled as hit squads for such occasions as the transfer of the ashes of the reviled Zola to the Panthéon. But popular antimilitarism was also stimulated. An International Antimilitarist Association was set up at Amsterdam in 1904. It had links with anarchists, the CGT, and socialists like Gustave Hervé who argued that the workers had no country but their class and should respond to any mobilization order by a general strike. The authorities clamped down heavily on such people, twenty-eight of whom, including Hervé were sent for trial in December 1905 for attempting to subvert conscripts. However antimilitarism was not the same as antipatriotism, and while the CGT committed itself to launching a general strike against war the SFIO was keen to demonstrate its patriotism. Jaurès himself was an antimilitarist, in that he opposed long-service armies which could be used to stage *coups d'état*, to put down strikes and to start colonial wars; but – not least to maintain links with the Radicals – he tried to reconcile socialism and patriotism. France, he said, was the *patrie* – the land of liberty – and must be defended against invasion not for chauvinistic French interests but for the benefit of Humanity. The workers had been at the forefront of national defence in 1792–3 and 1870–1, while aristocrats and bourgeois treated with the enemy. And the more socialists achieved reforms in France, the more France would become the patrimony of the working class. Antimilitarism and patriotism could be reconciled if France organized a citizen army which would defend the *patrie* but would not let itself be used for strike-breaking, *coups* or wars of aggression. This was the burden of Jaurès's book, *L'Armée nouvelle*, in 1910.

While the Left was able to reconcile the revolutionary tradition and patriotism, the Right was able to reconcile Catholicism and patriotism. Joan of Arc had long been celebrated by the Right as one sent by God to restore France to Catholicism and (for Maurras) to reinvigorate the monarchy, while the anticlerical Left argued that Joan had been burned by the Church and was a martyr to its intolerance. On the other hand, the rallying of Catholics to the Republic and its renewed greatness and the exhaustion of the anticlerical campaign after the Separation of Church and state made it possible to portray Joan of Arc as a republican, Catholic and national heroine all at once and a symbol of France acceptable to both Right and Left [195; 198 *pp. 156–60*].

Barrès was led by his cult of blood and soil to realize that the French past was Catholic, symbolized by its cathedrals, and that the Catholicism of Alsace-Lorraine (ignoring its Lutheran and Jewish populations) had for forty years been the most important factor preventing its full integration into the German Reich. Interest in the lost provinces revived, stimulated by plays and writings including Barrès's cycle of novels, *Les Bastions de l'Est*, and Hansi's best-selling illustrated history of Alsace, in which the Germans all have red noses. But the interest in Alsace-Lorraine was above all in France. The foundation of a Catholic university at Strasbourg in 1902, insulation against Combist persecution, and a constitution in 1911 which enlarged both provincial and federal representation effectively reconciled the inhabitants of Alsace-Lorraine to the Reich [213].

The second Morocco crisis of 1911–12 seemed to be a gift to the Right. Caillaux preserved the peace and Morocco for the French by ceding some of the French Congo but was then chased from office on the grounds that he had failed to protect French interests. Nationalist agitation reached a peak both in France and Germany [214]. Maurras published a pamphlet called *Kiel and Tangiers*, in which he argued that the monarchy had to be restored if France were to stand up to Germany. Albert de Mun, who had been instrumental in the fall of Caillaux, was also instrumental in the rise of Poincaré to the presidency of the Republic [215], and he exacted notable concessions for Catholics along the way. This did not mean that the Right was obtaining power through the back door. Poincaré strengthened the presidency by the force of his character and because foreign relations, which were the president's affair, had become all-important. But Maurras's argument was correspondingly weakened. Poincaré as President of the Republic, observed Péguy, was a republican monarch; with him the French had all the advantages of monarchy and none of the risks. Moreover, Poincaré's ministers, though moderate, had impeccable republican credentials. Not even when war broke out in 1914 was a non-republican of any shade given office (although one or two names were considered).

The overthrow of Barthou in December 1913 and the defeat of his party in April 1914 was a blow to Poincaré's system. The Radicals and SFIO triumphed with the commitment to abrogate the three-year military service law and put progressive income tax on the statute book. The ex-socialist Viviani became Prime Minister. But given the international crisis, the ministry agreed to retain the three-year law if the Senate agreed to progressive income tax. Poincaré went to St Petersburg to ensure the solidarity of Russia. Popular opinion (when the end of Madame Caillaux's trial allowed it to focus on events outside France), was massively hostile to Austrian aggression, supported by Germany, in the Balkans. If the CGT and SFIO had wanted to resist war by a general strike, they would have been swept away. Instead, they rallied to the defence of the Republic [*Doc. 20*] [216; 217; 218; 219]. Guesde, the revolutionary, accepted office. In the face of the enemy all classes and all parties rallied in what was dubbed the *Union Sacrée* [220]. The check inflicted on the German advance on the Marne in September was widely seen as a miracle which demonstrated that Joan of Arc was indeed watching over France, Catholics and republicans alike. The conflicts of the Third Republic were suspended, not resolved, but for the moment France was united, and in the course of the next four years, republic would avenge itself against monarchy on the battlefield.

PART THREE: CONCLUSION

10 THE THIRD REPUBLIC ASSESSED

The Third Republic has never had a very good press. It is often seen as one of those liberal, democratic regimes like Weimar Germany which, although tolerant and well-meaning, was unable to withstand the challenge of less savoury politics and more aggressive neighbours. The Republic, it is true, crumbled before the tanks and air-power of Nazi Germany in 1940, and the life of the Republic after the Great War was no doubt less happy than it had been before 1914. However, this should not blind us to the clear evidence that before 1914 the Third Republic was a viable government and a stable society.

Three criticisms are regularly made of the Third Republic. First, that under it France was a backward country economically, at least by western European standards. Second, that it was politically unstable and riven by outdated ideological quarrels. And third, that the Republic was by nature unpatriotic and a weakling in the society of nations.

The first criticism is that France was economically backward. France's population was increasing very slowly, and in 1911 was 39 million to Germany's 65 million. France was described as a peasant society, one of small, inefficient farms and sleepy villages. It was said that industrial workers were recruited from the countryside and dreamed of returning there to raise hens and rabbits. Industry counted for little in the gross national product, and was characterized by artisans making luxury articles and family firms in which the business existed to maintain the family rather than the other way round. It was a country without a proletariat, and France was a society of *rentiers*, who invested their savings, not in industry, but in government stock and above all in land. The ambition of the *bourgeois* was to retire to the countryside and relax on the income from his vineyard [221].

This view is partly a nostalgic self-image of the French, that of Marcel Pagnol and Gabriel Chevallier's *Clochemerle* (1934), and partly the view of American scholars like Laurence Wylie who discovered France after the Second World War [222], and were charmed by a society so different from their own. There is a danger that remembrance of things past will become caricature, and it is as well to recall some of the more dynamic features of French economic life. Agriculture was clearly in the doldrums, with a growth-rate of 0.5 per cent per annum between 1880 and 1913. But after the depression of the 1880s, there was a spurt of 1 per cent per annum between 1895 and 1913, which was as high as in the prosperous middle decades of the century, and farm incomes rose markedly after 1895, largely in response to rising demand from the towns. In industry, similarly, between the 1860s and the end of the century there was a slackening of growth, which averaged about 1.5 per cent per annum. But after 1895, and particularly between 1906 and 1929, there was an economic *Belle Epoque* during which industrial growth amounted to 5 per cent per annum.

Industrialization may not have been characterized by huge coalfields and giant factories, but success was marked in new industries such as engineering, electricals and chemicals, and labour productivity was higher in this period in France than in Germany [223]. The old crafts of the artisans became high-tech enterprises, as when carriage-making mutated into the automobile industry. In 1913 France was making 45,000 vehicles a year. New sources of power were being developed to supply these new industries, particularly hydroelectric power in the Alpine region around Grenoble. The engineers trained by France's élite technical schools moved aggressively into the private sector after 1890, headed the new industries and undertook vast projects such as the electrification of the transport and lighting systems of Paris. And though industry continued to be 80 per cent self-financing, banks were becoming much more interested in industrial investment, and between 1895 and 1906 industry's share of the stock issue on the Paris Stock Exchange rose from half to two-thirds [224].

The second main accusation brought against the Republic is that it was politically unstable. In particular, it is demonstrated that ministries came and went in the Italian style, and that France lacked strong leadership. The truth is that France had made a deliberate choice against both monarchy and Empire, which at various times since the Revolution had shown contempt for constitutional, parliamentary forms of government. The Third Republic was a parliamentary Republic and designed as such. The president was elected by parliament and was not allowed to dissolve the Chamber of

Deputies without the agreement of the Senate precisely so that the *coup d'état* of 1851 should not happen again. There was continuity in the predominance of a certain political class which threw up men of undoubted quality: Jules Ferry, René Waldeck-Rousseau, and Théophile Delcassé, to name but a few. When a more presidential style was appropriate, as on the eve of the First World War, parliament found a man who clearly had the weight and authority to be an assertive president, Raymond Poincaré. Georges Clemenceau, remembered by history as the Tiger, was in fact one of the most destructive politicians of the Third Republic, known in the 1880s as the 'toppler of ministries'. It says much that he was denied the highest office, but that Poincaré, who disliked and mistrusted Clemenceau, nevertheless appreciated his undoubted quality and asked him to form a government to win the war in 1917.

Criticism of the parliamentary nature of the Republic tends to focus either on the rule of party or on the alleged corruption of the regime. But it should be remembered that this criticism was not always objective, and was often motivated by particular interest. One scathing critic of the rule of party, for example, was General de Gaulle, who resigned from the provisional government of the Fourth Republic in 1946 because the parties were about to make another parliamentary constitution. But that system worked so well that De Gaulle was not called back from the political wilderness until the Algerian problem finished off the Fourth Republic twelve years later. Even then, in framing the constitution of the Fifth Republic in 1958, he was careful not to reject indirect elections to the presidency which had been enshrined since 1875, for fear that memories of 1848 and 1851 would be revived. When he did institute direct presidential elections in 1962, they were indeed revived. There was always a broad body of support for the parliamentary republic, and not only from politicians.

Attacks on the corruption of the Third Republic – and in particular on the manipulation of politicians by finance and the press – were very common at the time. Maupassant, for instance, exposed it cleverly in his novel *Bel Ami* (1885). Yet many of these criticisms came from members of the Right like Maurice Barrès, who had been excluded from power by the republican political class. Their bitterness was in part the sour grapes of those who had been cast out of the charmed circles of political patronage since the events of 1877.

The absence of *alternance* in power between Left and Right was a fundamental fact of political life in the Third Republic and an option that was deliberately excluded by the republicans [20]. This is a much more promising target for attack, and it is worth investigating whether anything can be said in defence of the Republic's exclusivism.

The first justification is that the battle was fought in the realm of ideology, not of force. During the First Republic, the republicans had resorted to force in 1795 and 1797 when the royalists threatened to win parliamentary elections. Under the constitution of 1875 the royalists never came near to winning a parliamentary majority. The republicans accused them of plotting counter-revolution; but this was by and large a rhetorical device, which served the cause of raising the spectre of tithes and feudal dues before the eyes of the peasantry and thus induced them to support the Republic. Positive benefits accrued also, such as universal suffrage, free elementary education, and railway branch lines. During the election campaign of 1885 Jules Ferry declared that the republicans had won the democratic support of the countryside, and reminded his audience that the peasants owed their untroubled property rights to the Revolution.

The ideology of Jacobinism, which placed the regime, the Catholic Church and the army at the centre of political debate and excluded other issues – especially social issues – from consideration, has been seen as the sterile reworking of arguments which rightfully belonged to the French Revolution. There is some truth in this. The claims of the working class and women were repeatedly subordinated to the pursuit of traditional quarrels. Just when it seemed that new issues were forcing their way to the front – in the 1890s, for example – the Dreyfus Affair drove the politicians back to familiar battle lines.

However, it would be untrue to say that the Third Republic enacted no social programme. Women's rights in matters of education, property and marriage were extended, even if the vote eluded them before 1945. Trade-union rights, factory acts, accident insurance and pensions were established for the working classes, paid for by progressive taxes on inheritance and income. Some price had to be paid for the entry of radicals and socialists into the Jacobin coalition. Sometimes that price was too high, and it seemed as if the republicans would relax the rules of republican legitimacy and enter a partnership with the moderate Right. There were signs of this under Rouvier in 1887, and under Méline in 1896–8. Poincaré was elected president with support from the Right. Many politicians who bore the label of the Left were effectively on the Right in terms of the policies they pursued. Clemenceau was the great strike-breaker of 1906–8, Caillaux as leader of the Senate was the arch-enemy of the Popular Front in the 1930s, Millerand became a conservative president of the Republic after the war, and the working-class constituents of Briand used to read his early anarchist speeches at uproarious drinking parties. But politicians of the traditional Right, however liberal they became, never gained office before 1914, and the return of the Right had to await what Maurras called the 'divine surprise' of 1940.

Before the First World War the republican political class was able to play on its revolutionary heritage to keep the labour movement bound tightly in alliance, and when that failed, it could bend its own rules to make some sort of working compromise with the Right. Both of these options became more difficult in the wake of the Bolshevik Revolution of 1917. On the one hand, the Communist Party broke with the Socialist Party and ballooned on the extreme left. (The socialists, instead of becoming more 'social democratic', in fact moved further to the left in pursuit of the same voters as the Communists: the socialists refused to enter a government with the Radicals until 1936.) On the other hand, Bolshevism created its own enemy at the opposite end of the political spectrum – Fascism. Even if French Fascism was not on the same scale and of the same nature as Fascism in Italy or Germany, it transformed the nature of the Right in France and ruled out bridge-building on the model of the *Ralliement*.

The third criticism of the Third Republic is that it was unpatriotic and not quite a Great Power. At various times before 1914, Catholics were accused of being more loyal to the Papacy than to France and of being happy to see the godless Republic roundly chastized; intellectuals were accused of undermining the army and thus the ability of France to defend itself; primary school teachers were accused of inculcating antipatriotic sentiments in the classroom; and workers were accused of planning a general strike and revolution in the event of war being declared. However, these accusations tended to derive from groups which sought to appropriate a monopoly of nationalism and to denounce their opponents as defeatists. There was a patriotism of the Left and one of the Right. The Dreyfusard intellectuals wanted a France which would defend the Rights of Man, and not subordinate them to *raison d'état*. Anti-militarism and even anti-imperialism did not necessarily entail antipatriotism. The workers were ready to leap to the defence of France against the 'Boches'. On the Left the defence of France meant the defence of the Republic. The Right was critical of the Republic and keen to demonstrate that France was more than the Republic. After the Separation of Church and State, it was easier to argue that Catholicism was a potent ingredient of French national consciousness and Joan of Arc was duly acclaimed as a national heroine, republican and French as well as Catholic. In August 1914, unlike in May–June 1940, France held together. The International was washed away by the tide of popular patriotism, anticlerical legislation was suspended, and chaplains accompanied the infantrymen to the front. The *Union Sacrée* was established.

Neither did France demonstrate any great weakness in 1914. The first onslaught of the German military was checked on the Marne in September and the Schlieffen Plan – which for a generation had projected a war by timetable by which Germany could defeat France *and* Russia – was consigned to the rubbish-tip of history. The fortress of Verdun was held in 1916. The German offensive of 1918 was again stopped on the Marne. Between 1914 and 1918 France mobilized 8.4 million men, thousands of whom were carried to the front by 'the taxis of the Marne'. It was a war fought by the French people. 1.35 million died and 3.5 million were wounded; nearly 60 per cent of those mobilized were killed or wounded [225]. There is scarcely a village in France without its war memorial, more often than not one showing a *poilu* (as the infantryman was called) sinking into the flag. By comparison Great Britain and the United States lost 950,000 and 100,000 men respectively. In 1919, in the Hall of Mirrors of the Chateau of Versailles, France redeemed the humiliating defeat of 1870 and the proclamation of the German Empire in that same hall in 1871, and imposed a resounding peace – including the recovery of Alsace-Lorraine – on the successor of the German Empire, the Weimar Republic.

PART FOUR: DOCUMENTS

Note: all texts except 1(b) have been translated by the author.

DOCUMENT 1   TWO VIEWS OF POPULAR SOVEREIGNTY

Republicans stood for popular sovereignty but had to reckon with the fact that universal suffrage was upheld by the Second Empire. The main dispute with the Empire and among liberals and republicans was how that popular sovereignty should be exercised. In document (a), Gambetta tells his electors of Belleville, in the Paris suburbs, of the need to organize a firm parliamentary Left to establish responsible, but still parliamentary, government. In document (b), on the eve of the Commune, the central committee of delegates from vigilance committees in each of the twenty arrondissements of Paris shows itself suspicious of all parliamentary representation.

(a) We must organise a Left, composed exclusively of citizens who have rallied to the same principles.

The idea is not to purge but to make uniform; we must decompose the current Left into two parts and between them draw a line of demarcation which from now on will prevent confusion, without ruling out good-neighbourly relations and occasional co-operation.

The first fraction includes the supporters of constitutional monarchy. All those who believe that universal suffrage may be reconciled with *necessary liberties* must put themselves under the orders of M. Thiers and his friends, and resolutely pursue the restoration of pure parliamentarism. The other fraction will now be made up uniquely of those who think that the people is the only true and only legitimate sovereign, but that it requires the reality of power; those who, with Favre, Simon, Bancel, Pelletan, and the others think and say that the people will be satisfied only when they have demoted their masters to the rank of fully obedient and responsible subalterns ...

In short, they believe that the country will have neither order, security or liberty until a fully emancipated universal suffrage has founded democratic institutions which of themselves will ensure liberty, equality and fraternity.

Letter of Gambetta to the electors of the first constituency of the Seine, 28 July 1869, in *Discours et Plaidoyers politiques*, vol. i, Paris, 1881, pp. 432–3.

(b) Every member of a vigilance committee declares his adherence to the Revolutionary-Socialist Party. Consequently he demands and seeks to obtain by all means possible the elimination of the privileges of the bourgeoisie, its elimination as a governing caste, and the assumption of political power by the workers. In a word: social equality. No more employers, no more proletariat, no more classes. He recognises labour as the sole foundation of the social order and believes that the full product of labour should belong to the worker.

In the area of politics he places the existence of the Republic above the question of majority rule. Consequently he does not recognise the right of any majority to deny the principle of popular sovereignty, whether by plebiscite or indirectly, or by any assembly that would represent such a majority. He will therefore oppose, by force if necessary, the convocation of any constituent or alleged National Assembly that would occur before the foundations of the present social order have been altered decisively through political and social revolutionary change.

Until this definitive revolution shall have occurred, he recognises as the government of the city only the revolutionary Commune emanating from the delegation of the revolutionary-socialist groups of this same city.

Declaration of principles of the Delegation of the Twenty *Arrondissements*, 19 February 1871, in Eugene Schulkind, *The Paris Commune of 1871*, 1972, pp. 90–1.

DOCUMENT 2   TWO VIEWS OF ROYALIST RESTORATION

The main obstacle in the way of a royalist restoration was the gulf which separated the Pretender in exile from the royalist politicians in France. Document (a) is the famous manifesto of the Comte de Chambord on 5 July 1871; document (b) is a programme drawn up by the royalist majority of the National Assembly, hammered together in difficult negotiations between the royalist factions, but rejected by Chambord.

(a) No, just because the ignorant and credulous have spoken of privileges, absolutism, intolerance and, what else? Of tithes and feudal dues, spectres which the most audacious bad faith is trying to raise before your eyes, I will not let the standard of Henri IV, of Francis I and of Joan of Arc be snatched from my grasp. With that flag national unity was achieved. I received it like a sacred trust from the old king, my forefather [Charles X], dying in exile. For me it has always been inseparable from the memory of my absent country; it has floated over my cradle, and I wish it to shade my tomb. I will bring you order and liberty in the glorious folds of this unsullied standard. People of France! Henri V cannot abandon the white flag of Henri IV.

Manifesto of the Comte de Chambord, 5 July 1871, cited in Comte de Falloux, *Mémoires d'un Royaliste*, vol. II, Paris, 1888, pp. 481–2.

(b) We consider monarchy to be the natural government of the country, and by monarchy we understand traditional hereditary monarchy. Monarchy has made France, and for centuries given her stability and greatness. In 1789 it anticipated reforms spontaneously, and in 1814 it both founded liberty and safeguarded territorial integrity. A hereditary, representative, constitutional monarchy assures the country the right to participate in the running of its own affairs, and under the guarantee of ministerial responsibility assures all the necessary liberties – political, civil, religious, equality before the law, free access to all professions, to all honours and to all social advantages, and the peaceful and continuous improvement of the condition of the working classes.

Programme of the Right, cited in Duc d'Audiffret-Pasquier, *La Maison de France et l'Assemblée Nationale. Souvenirs, 1871–1873*, Paris, 1938, pp. 54–5.

DOCUMENT 3   A CONSERVATIVE REPUBLIC?

In this address to the National Assembly the consummate politician, Thiers, tries to establish the Republic as a regime beyond questioning by the Right, but at the same time warns that anarchy and radical party politics will serve only to improve the chances of Bonapartism. His plea is for a sober parliamentary Republic which will represent the Nation.

The Republic exists, it is the legal government of the country; to want anything else would be a new revolution and the most fearful of all. Let us not waste time declaring it; but use the time to impress upon it desirable and necessary characteristics. A commission appointed by you a few months ago gave it the title of conservative Republic. Let us seize that title and strive to deserve it. (*'Hear, hear!'*)

Every government must be conservative and no society can live under a government which is not. (*General agreement.*) The Republic will be conservative, or it will not exist. (*Exclamations.*)

A VOICE ON THE CENTRE LEFT: Hear, hear! We'll buy that!

THE PRESIDENT OF THE REPUBLIC: France does not want to live in continual crisis. She wishes to live at peace, to work to feed herself and to meet the huge obligations [German reparations] placed upon her. And if she is not given the peace she so badly needs, the government which fails to give her peace, whatever it is, will not long be tolerated! (*'That's right!' 'Hear, hear!'* on a large number of benches on the left and centre left.) Let us have no illusions. It may be thought that it is possible to found a republic which is that of a party, based on the power of the many, thanks to universal suffrage. Such a republic would not last a day.

Even the many need rest, security and work. (*'That's right!' 'Hear, hear!'*) ... Having made others afraid, they become afraid of themselves, throw themselves into the arms of an opportunist dictator and pay for a few days of disastrous licence with twenty years of slavery. (*'That's right, that's right!' Prolonged applause on many benches.*)

Yes, let us break the chain which links these two evil opposites, and make peace instead of disorder. Let us make the necessary sacrifices for general security, even sacrifices which may seem excessive, and above all let us not so much as glimpse the rage of party.

The Revolution of 1789 was made so that there would be no more classes, so that in the nation there would be only the nation itself, living entirely under the same law, bearing the same burdens, enjoying the same advantages, in which all, in a word, were rewarded or punished according to their deeds. (*'Hear, hear!' and applause on the left.*)

For myself, I understand and accept the Republic only as it should be, as a government of the nation which, having for a long time and in good faith left the direction of its destinies to a hereditary power, which failed as a result of mistakes which we cannot assess today, decides to run its own affairs itself, through deputies freely and wisely elected, not according to party, or class, or origin, taking them neither from the top or the bottom, neither from the left nor the right, but in the light of public esteem, where character, qualities, defects cannot be mistaken, and choosing them with a freedom that can be enjoyed only in the midst of order, calm and security. (*Bravos and approval – acclamations – on the left.*)

Adolphe Thiers, Speech to National Assembly, 13 November 1872, *Journal Officiel de la République Française*, 14 November 1872, pp. 6,981–2.

DOCUMENT 4   THE ESTABLISHMENT OF REPUBLICAN
            LEGITIMACY

In this speech on 16 June 1877, a month after the coup of 16 May and the day on which the Chamber of Deputies was dissolved by the President of the Republic with the approval of the Senate, Gambetta firmly denounces the Right as supporters of the old regime. It is a statement of republican legitimacy, in which those who claim the heritage of the French Revolution disqualify from office in the Republic those whom they argue cannot do so.

M. GAMBETTA – I am asking you whether the constitution has closed the era of revolutions, yes or no. Messieurs, I am fully aware – and this is precisely the grievance I am expressing about the ministers – I know only too well that those devoted servants of the policy of 16 May are the sworn enemies of the constitution. It is just that some dare not say it while others say and proclaim it daily. (*Applause on the left.*)

... We are confronted by men who are not rooted in the constitution. These are not men who defend the constitution with their own particular style, though still in harmony with the spirit of the constitution. No! No! If that were the case, if there were a Whig party and a Tory party in the Republic, we could debate and engage in parliamentary politics. We could believe that the President has nothing but constitutional sentiments. But everyone knows that this is not the case. Everyone knows that it would be impossible for you [on the Right] to say with sincerity that there is a single one among you who does not have a political ideal different from· that which governs us today. (*Loud approval on the left.*)

Oh, Messieurs, make no mistake ... it does not befit you, given your origins, to speak of the principles of 1789 (*Ironic outbursts on the left*) and to say that you favour equality. It would be something to hear you say here that you favour ducal supremacy and the oligarchy of a few nobles. ('*Hear, hear!' on the left.*)

Ah! You say that you endorse the French Revolution! In that case I will declare before the country that you can be called only one thing: you are called the counter-revolution. ('*Hear, hear!' on the left and centre.*) You can bear nothing but that name because today, as in 1830 ... we are confronted by nobles who will not accept democracy, and by a congregation [the Jesuit order] which wants to enslave France. (*Bravos and applause on the left.*)

Léon Gambetta, Speech to the Chamber of Deputies, 16 June 1877, in *Discours et Plaidoyers politiques de Gambetta*, vol. vii, Paris, 1882, pp. 125–6, 140.

DOCUMENT 5   TWO VIEWS OF PARLIAMENTARY LIFE

The parliamentary system of the Third Republic came in for a good deal of criticism. One of its most scathing critics was Maurice Barrès, a Boulangist in his youth, who later wrote a series of novels against the regime: Les Déracinés, L'Appel au Soldat, *and* Leurs Figures. *In document (a), an extract from the second novel, he puts the words of criticism into the mouth of the radical, later Boulangist, politician Naquet. But the parliamentary system must have been in the interests of many people, as Robert de Jouvenel explains in document (b), from* La République des Camarades, *originally published in 1914.*

(a) The evil lies in parliamentary institutions. A regime which places ministers in the Chamber sterilises them; we are for ever discussing not what is on the order paper but the fall or survival of the cabinet. The question of confidence is posed at every step, which perverts all debates and inhibits the free vote. How can deputies be free when ministers force them to opt between a vote for them and a ministerial crisis? Which deputy would refuse to support a minister from whom he was requesting the gift of tax collectorships or tobacconists' licences? And how can he avoid making these requests when electors know the decisive influence of a deputy on the choice of ministers and insist that he gets to work for them on pain of non-re-election? Private interests take precedence over the public interest and the administration falls apart. The way to end this deplorable state of affairs would be to separate administration from legislation, to confine parliament to making laws and let ministers enforce them. That, sirs, is what we are going to do with General Boulanger.

Maurice Barrès, *L'Appel au Soldat*, Livre de Poche, p. 122.

(b) When you become a deputy, you can have only one pressing preoccupation: to remain one.

The difficulty varies between constituency and constituency. In some regions, it is enough to hold the office in order to keep it.

'That deputy is already well greased,' say electors in some distant provinces, whereas of a new one they say, 'he will have to be greased.'

I'm not sure whether that isn't the last word of wisdom, so far as universal suffrage is concerned.

Elsewhere, on the other hand, they like new faces. There it is most difficult to keep one's seat.

To keep your seat, there is only one essential rule: think about it all the time. The deputy who is always thinking about it must divide his time between three principal tasks: running errands, making promises, and writing.

If his errands bear no fruit, if his promises are always empty and if his letters never achieve anything definitive, that is only of minor importance. The elector who requests a service does not always insist on the deputy delivering. He wants 1. to demonstrate his importance; and 2. to receive letters.

A good deputy, who receives a letter from an elector, must straightaway write three:

One to the competent administration, to pass on the request of the interested party.

One to the interested party, to notify him that his request is being dealt with.

A second to the same, to advise him of the decision of the competent administration.

Deputies who receive forty letters a day from electors are not exceptional.

Parliament does not reign, does not govern, it writes. The regime which presides over our destinies is neither the Republic, nor the Empire, nor Royalty, nor autocracy, nor democracy – it is Correspondence.

Robert de Jouvenel, *La République des Camarades*, Bernard Grasset, Paris, 1934, pp. 22–4.

DOCUMENT 6   ANTICLERICALISM: RHETORIC AND
                REALISM

*These two documents illustrate different faces of anticlericalism. Document
(a) is a speech by Gambetta on the campaign in the south of France, not
long after the 16 May crisis, which is clearly appreciated by his left-wing,
robustly anticlerical audience. Document (b), from a speech delivered in
parliament ten years later by the architect of the education reforms, Jules
Ferry, is an attempt to stop anticlericalism short of the hurdle of
disestablishment. He is attacked by the Left but can do nothing to gain the
confidence of the Right.*

(a) I am going to tackle a question which attracts passion and vehemence:
the clerical question, the question of relations between Church and State. It
is indeed a huge question, because it holds all other questions in suspense,
because ... within it lies the question of hostility to modern thought and the
conflict which we have to resolve.

What has not been said on this issue? The inviolable domain of our
consciences has been invaded and attempts have been made to interpret our
policies in the dim light of our philosophy. I no more accept this position
than I would accept that I can grasp the intimate sentiments of the religious
conscience of a political adversary in order to attack his political standpoint.
Even so I have the right to denounce the peril that is threatening French
society, as it is constituted and as it wishes to be, from the growth of a
spirit that is not merely clerical, but Vaticanesque, monastic, congregationist
and syllabist [a reference to the Papal Syllabus of Errors of 1864]. It is a
spirit that does not fear to subject the human mind to the crudest
fabrications, disguised by the most subtle and profound arguments, which
are those of ignorance trying to exploit slavishness in order to anchor itself.
(*Long bursts of applause. Bravos and repeated shouts of: 'Long live
Gambetta'.*)

... I do not simply want to take things from the point of view of party,
which I do not recognise as valid for anyone, but from the governmental,
public, and national point of view. In the light of ceaseless encroachment
and usurpation by the clerical mind which is served by 40,000 regulars on
top of the secular clergy, I have the right to say as I expose those masters of
deceit who talk of the social peril: *there* is the social peril! (*Bursts of
applause. Signs of unanimous agreement.*)

Léon Gambetta, speech at Romans, 18 September 1878, in *Discours et
Plaidoyers politiques de Gambetta*, vol. viii, Paris, 1883, pp. 242–3.

(b) M. JULES FERRY – Messieurs, we remain profoundly attached to the lay
school; and yet as I have had occasion to say in various circumstances and
as I do not hesitate to say in this Assembly, we are most anxious to see
religious peace reign in this country. (*Loud exclamations on the left.
Applause in the centre.*)

M. LE COMTE DE MUN – Mr Speaker, I have restrained myself for three hours, I have not interrupted, but I surely have the right to say to the speaker that he is the last person here who can talk about religious peace. (*'Hear, hear!' on the right.*)

M. JULES FERRY – Messieurs, there are three questions in this country which concern religious peace: the question of religious associations, the question of the state subsidy of the churches, and the school question.

M. BASLY [Socialist, Paris] – Vote the abolition of the subsidy.

M. JULES FERRY – The associations, Messieurs, were about ten years ago one of the noisiest episodes in what you call the war of religion. From time to time public authorities have to defend themselves, and then ... (*'Hear, hear!' on the left. Ironic comments and noise on the right.*) people say they have declared war on religion. At a certain moment we had to enforce the laws of the State and insist that the religious congregations observe existing laws and decrees. (*'Hear, hear!' on the left. Interruptions on the right.*)

... There is, Messieurs, a second point, a second question which stirs up and heats debate and delays the establishment of religious peace in this country: the question of the state subsidy of the churches. On this matter my personal feelings are well known to everyone in this assembly. I support the state subsidy. I know very well that my honourable colleagues on this side [the extreme left] think that the abolition of the subsidy will better contribute to public peace.

If I believed that the separation of Church and State, the abolition of the subsidy, would serve public peace in this country, I would vote with them. (*Interruptions on the left.*) But I am profoundly convinced that far from pacifying religious disputes, this abolition would spread them into the tiniest village ... (*'Hear, hear!' on the right. Interruptions on the extreme left.*) Messieurs, I have said nothing new and unexpected, and I would wish to be allowed to express myself freely ... I believe that far from strengthening the state, the abolition of the subsidy would weaken it and strengthen only passions. (*'Hear, hear!' on various benches.*) ... As for the lay schools, as for the separation of Church and school, I deny absolutely that, whether in law or in practice, it had the character of religious persecution which you attribute to it. (*Interruptions on the right and extreme left.*)

M. FERROUL [Radical-socialist, Aude] – You will be a cardinal before Jules Simon.

Speech of Jules Ferry to the Chamber of Deputies, 6 June 1889, in Jules Ferry, *Discours et Opinions*, vol. iv, Paris, 1896, pp. 475–8.

DOCUMENT 7   BOULANGISM

One way to discredit Boulanger was to tar him with the brush of Bonapartism; but in this speech, document (a), to an audience of Bonapartists, Boulanger proclaims his republicanism and his desire to open the Republic to those ejected beyond the pale of republican legitimacy. In his reply to Boulanger, document (b), Ferry wields the tar-brush again, and calls for republican unity against Boulanger. But he is anxious to win back radicals from Boulanger without conceding any of their criticisms of the parliamentary Republic.

(a) If I have attracted along with republican votes the votes of men who, in serving fallen regimes, also served the country, and those of electors who have remained faithful to names which, while they recall our misfortunes, recall also our glories, it is not because these men did me the injury of supposing that in spite of my republican protestations I wanted to restore one of the former regimes. It is rather that, instructed by experience, they are in agreement with me and, may I say also, with you, in wanting a new, national Republic, open to all honest men and to every progress made by the people, for the people, and in which the people would have not only the too frequently illusory right to express their wishes, but the power to realise them ... If we are beginning our history again, it is to go back not to 1851, but rather to 1789.

Speech of Boulanger to the Bonapartist Committee of the Nièvre department, on 2 December 1888, anniversary of the *coup d'état* of Louis-Napoleon in 1851. Cited by Odile Rudelle, *La République absolue, 1870–1889*, Paris, 1982, p. 230.

(b) The innovators today are the most dismal and unsentimental of plagiarisers. The men of 1789 are asleep in their silent grave. Those beating at the door are the men of Brumaire! (*Prolonged applause. Agitation.*)

What is threatened is perhaps not immediately the republican form of government. The dynastic principle in this country seems to be played out. The head of the house of France believes in restoration by plebiscite (*Laughter*) and the Bonapartists are flowing to Boulangism like water to the river. (*Renewed laughter.*)

What is threatened is something higher and deeper: that is liberty itself, the government of the country by the country, government by Assemblies, everything for which France has striven for thirty years of parliamentary monarchy and for twenty years of Republic, everything that has been the passion of our youth and the dignity of our middle age. That is what is in danger! (*Unanimous approval.*)

... On the eve of the great Centenary, doubt enters our hearts. If this evil continues and triumphs, if the blow falls, Messieurs, we will in this year 1889 be witness to the greatest, most abject and colossal forswearing of all that France has sought, loved, adored and served for a hundred years! (*Renewed applause.*)

But, Messieurs, that will not be ('*No! no!*') if all republicans, united this time, radicals and moderates, understand that the origin of the [Boulangist] movement is not in a surge of new ideas and odd reforms; if they understand that the origin is elsewhere, in the lassitude of the nation, the need for peace and good government that France feels; if they understand that the duty of everyone, radical and moderate, is to work together for the restoration of the principles, traditions and practice of government in this country. (*Loud cheers.*)

... There are things we cannot do. We want the union of republicans, but we cannot and must not join together on the territory of the radicals. (*General agreement.*)

Can we accept revision?

I myself make very little distinction between the different shades of revisionist. There are those who want only to remove the prerogatives of the president of the Republic and the dignity of the Senate. I personally think that they are no different from those who want fairly and squarely to abolish the Senate and the presidency. ('*Hear, hear!*')

Revision, besides, you see, Messieurs, by the logic of ideas and realities, is not just the abolition of the presidency and the Senate. It is worse than that: a Constituent Assembly. ('*Yes! yes!*' '*Hear, hear!*')

... In all kinds of folly the best thing is not to start at all. We are not revisionists, not in the least. We think that there is nothing which needs revision in the constitution at the moment. We will tell the electorate such, and we will stand before it against the revisionist party which draws together all the enemies of the constitutional Republic. (*Loud applause.*)

Speech by Jules Ferry to the Republican Association, 21 December 1888, in Jules Ferry, *Discours et Opinions*, vol. vi, Paris, 1898, pp. 126–8.

DOCUMENT 8   REVOLUTION OR REFORM?

These passages illustrate one element of the internal debate among socialists: how to achieve the socialist society. In document (a) the Marxist, Jules Guesde, whose party has scored successes at recent municipal and parliamentary elections, is reluctant to shed the label of revolutionary socialism. Document (b) is part of a lengthy address to the court by the young anarchist Émile Henry after being sentenced to death; he was guillotined a month later. Document (c) is from a pamphlet by another anarchist, Fernand Pelloutier, who sees no purpose in individual acts of terrorism, but argues that if anarchists find working-class support and convert it into a revolutionary general strike, they can defeat the forces of the bourgeois state.

(a) Far from being mutually exclusive, electoral action and revolutionary action are complementary and have always been complementary in our country, where for all parties victorious insurrection has always followed and capped the vote.

Today socialism is legalist and electoralist in the same sense as all parties which have gone before and which are now combined against it with what strength they have left.

There is and will only be a single set of means to the end in view, which are determined by circumstance. Where a revolution is the end those means are always revolutionary. The ballot is revolutionary, however legal it may be, when it organises Labour against Capital and fights elections on the battleground of class. Parliamentary action is revolutionary, however party-political it may be, when its oratory rallies the discontented of the workshop and counter and when it demonstrates that capitalist society is opposed to them or powerless to satisfy them.

Riot on the other hand is anti-revolutionary and reactionary, despite its illegality and violence, because it affords moribund capitalism the popular blood-letting it needs to survive and postpones the hour of deliverance.

Jules Guesde in *Le Socialiste*, 10 November 1894, cited in Jacques Droz (ed.), *Le Socialisme démocratique, 1864–1960*, Armand Colin, 1966, p. 76.

(b) It was then [after the failure of the Carmaux miners' strike] that I decided ... to add a voice that the bourgeois had heard before but believed had been silenced with Ravachol: that of dynamite.

I wanted to show the bourgeoisie that from now on it could have no unsullied pleasures, that its insolent victories would be undermined, that its golden calf would shake violently on its pedestal, until the final spasm which would topple it into slime and blood.

At the same time I wanted to show the miners that there was only one class of men, the anarchists, who felt for their suffering and were ready to avenge them. They had no seats in Parliament, like Monsieur Guesde and his consorts, yet they went to the guillotine.

... The bomb in the Café Terminus is the answer to your rape of liberty, your arrests, your house-searches, your press law, your mass expulsion of foreigners, your executions. But why, you ask, did I attack peaceful customers, who were listening to music, and were probably not magistrates, or deputies, or officials?

... Should we strike only the deputies who pass laws against us, the magistrates who enforce them and the police who arrest us?

I don't think so.

These men are only instruments who do not act in their own name; they are paid by the bourgeoisie for its own protection and are no more guilty than the rest.

The good bourgeois who have no official position but who cash their dividends and live idly on the profits created by the labour of workers should take their share of the reprisals.

And not only they but all those who are content with the existing order, who applaud the government's measures and are thus its accomplices, clerks on a salary of 300 to 500 francs a month who hate the people more than the rich bourgeois do, that stupid and conceited mass which sides always with the strongest, the usual clientele of the Terminus and other large cafés.

That is why I aimed into the crowd without choosing my victims.

Speech of Émile Henry at his trial, April 1894, in Jean Maitron, *Ravachol et les Anarchistes*, Collection Archives, Julliard, 1964, pp. 107, 109–10.

(c) SECOND WORKER: There would be the threat of revolt if not revolt itself everywhere at once. The government would have to freeze the garrisons. Instead of matching 30,000 insurgents with 100, 150 or 200,000 soldiers, in an area of about forty kilometres [25 miles] circumference, as in the classic revolution, the general strike would match 200,000 workers and 10,000 soldiers here, 10,000 and 500 there, or, as at Decazeville and Trignac, 1,000 or 1,200 against a brigade of gendarmerie. Can you see the difference? And look at the resources the strikers would have! Public transport would stop, street lights would go out, and it would be impossible to supply large centres ...

FIRST WORKER: That is certainly an improvement over previous revolutions I hadn't been aware of before. But wouldn't the Paris garrison alone be enough to crush the insurgents, given the modern weapons available?

SECOND WORKER: Of course, if the insurgents were stupid enough to mass at two or three central points. But that is precisely what would have to be avoided, and what the strikers would avoid, having everything to lose. They would remain in their neighbourhoods and take control there first of small workshops and bakeries, then of larger workshops, and finally, but only after the victory, of big industrial establishments. One of two things would happen. Either the government would divide its forces between the neighbourhoods involved and whereas previously the mass of soldiers crushed small groups of insurgents now the mass of insurgents would crush small groups of soldiers. Or the government would confine its troops to barracks and await some isolated and imprudent action by the strikers. But if such a localised and central action did not take place and if the takeover of the workshops were undertaken by small groups of men who remained dispersed and elusive, and the army were immobilised, how long do you think the government could keep it fed?

FIRST WORKER: Three months, I reckon.

SECOND WORKER: Not a fortnight ...

Fernand Pelloutier, 'Qu'est-ce que la grève générale?', cited in Jacques Julliard, *Fernand Pelloutier et les Origines du Syndicalisme d'Action Directe*, Seuil, 1971, pp. 326–7.

DOCUMENT 9   **THE** *RALLIEMENT*

The Ralliement *was an attempt by moderates on the Right to win the Opportunists away from the radicals in order to form a new majority based on the Centre Right and thus gain office. This is the thinking behind document (a), the manifesto of a new conservative republican party. However the Opportunists were reluctant to give any ground, and in document (b) the Prime Minister, Dupuy, brings out the spectre of the Right's intractable royalism in order to justify their monopoly of power.*

(a) Rest assured that we are no more now than then entering into open or covert conflict with the established regime. In our eyes the Republic is the legal government of the country. We have recognised it as such and we have no thought of retracting anything.

But there is a long way between recognising a government in principle and subscribing to the policies of the men in power.

Republican concentration has never been other than a war machine directed against conservative and liberal influences for the benefit of radicalism. It has had only one motto: 'clericalism, there is the enemy'; only one aim: the undisturbed appropriation of the Republic as private property; and only one method of government: the most intolerant exclusivism.

Our policy in view of uncertain but inevitable events has been to prepare the formation of a Tory Party bringing together as a constitutional opposition all those men of goodwill who are tired of the abuses and excesses of the party in power. The time had to come for the country ... to try while avoiding crisis to form a truly national government which would remain faithful to the democratic currents of our time but resolve firmly to uphold the claims of authority, respect for beliefs and the regular enjoyment of liberty. Our intention was not to be taken by surprise when the hour came, and events prove that we were not lacking in foresight.

It is our task to organise the democratic conservative party with a sincere loyalty. All those who wish to check the apostles of socialist neo-radicalism and masonic sectarians – and they are legion – will take their place in its ranks.

We have no excessive demands, harbour no suspicion or bitterness, peddle no metaphysical theories or vain idealism. We must make haste, forget our quarrels and put forward a single platform in these words: *for an open, tolerant, and honest Republic.*

Jacques Piou, Manifesto of the *Droite républicaine*, in *Le Figaro*, 8 January 1893.

(b) I recognise that unlike their ancestors they have learned something. But they will be the first to agree with me that they have forgotten nothing, not even the way to the royalist committees where doubtless they are planning some parallel action, or even a convergent one. I accept that they will endure the Republic; I am asking whether they would defend it!

Speech of Charles Dupuy at Toulouse, 23 May 1893, in Maxime Lecomte, *Les Ralliés. Histoire d'un parti, 1886–1898*, Paris, 1898, p. 233.

DOCUMENT 10   TWO VIEWS OF MÉLINE'S MINISTRY

Méline's government survived with the support of the Right, but the rules of republican legitimacy made it necessary for him to argue in document (a) that he was pursuing republican policies and held office by virtue of a truly republican majority. Not even someone as obviously conservative as Méline could admit to being on the Right. This hypocrisy is wittily exposed in document (b) by Anatole France, writing in 1901. The speaker, Henri Léon, vice-president of the royalist committees of the South-West, regrets the Méline era when, covertly if not openly, the Right was back in power.

(a) It is not enough to accuse a government of clericalism to demonstrate that it is clerical. You must prove it ... We are upholding the Concordat and the laws of state without being prejudiced or provocative, with a firm impartiality. ('*Hear, hear!*') The only thing we refuse to do is to declare war on religion itself, because even if France is not clerical, it is for the most part extremely tolerant. We have a sincere respect for religion, something which annoys the party that sees religion as a relic of servitude only to be destroyed.

No, we are not governing with the Right. To govern with a party means to execute its policy, its manifesto, or part of it at least. Our enemies know as well as we do that our policy is republican, clearly republican, and we make no concessions to anyone on this. Besides, no one has been so insolent as to ask us to.

The Right votes with us because it prefers our policy to that which is leading from radicalism to collectivism and because it places the interest of the country before its dynastic preferences. Or rather it does not vote with us so much as against social revolution, which it has every right to do.

As for our majority, I claim that it is the true republican majority, and I refer those who daily challenge us to the many division lists which prove it. Knock away the votes of the Right and then do the same thing for the opposing minority by knocking away the support of the socialists. You will find that the majority of republicans is with us, and in the country that majority is even stronger. (*Loud applause.*)

I know that in the radical camp they have tried to undermine this calculation by calling all those who are not republicans of long standing monarchist, and excommunicating those called scathingly the *ralliés*, as if it were not permitted after twenty-seven years of Republic to open our ranks to sincere and loyal men, like our colleague the Count of Alsace, all of whose votes since the beginning of the parliament have been as republican as our own. I do not hesitate to say that such support is an honour for the government and gives it more strength than certain revolutionary collectivists whose names I don't need to mention. Suffice it to say that without the support of the pure socialists the radical party would be in a minority of republicans and because of that it will not and cannot break with them.

Speech of Méline to his constituents at Remiremont, 10 October 1897, in Georges Lachapelle, Le Ministère Méline, J. L. L. d'Artrey, Paris, 1928, pp. 118–21.

(b) With Méline we had everything. We, the royalists, were in charge of the government, the army, the judiciary, the administration, the police ... Méline did us the immense service of giving us a reassuring air, of making us benign, benign, as benign as himself. He said that we were the republicans, and people believed him.

– With him, continued Henri Léon, we had everything, we were everything, we could do everything. We didn't even have to hide. We were not outside the Republic but above it. We dominated it from the heights of our patriotism. We were everyone who mattered, we were France. I am not soft on the whore [*la gueuse* – i.e. the Republic] but you have to admit she is sometimes good fun. Under Méline the police were exquisite, wonderful. Without exaggerating, they were wonderful. At a royalist demonstration which you kindly organised, Brécé, I shouted 'Up the police!' till I was hoarse. I meant it. The police were clouting the republicans smartly. Gérault-Richard was put in the cells for shouting: 'Long live the Republic!' Méline made life too easy for us. He was a real wet-nurse. He rocked us, he sent us to sleep. ... Happy times. Méline led the dance. Nationalists, monarchists, anti-Semites, plebiscitarians, we danced together to his village violin.

Anatole France, *M. Bergeret à Paris*, Calmann Levy, Livre de Poche, 1973, pp. 90–2.

DOCUMENT 11   INTELLECTUALS IN POLITICS

Blum's recollections of the Dreyfus Affair, written nearly forty years after the event, when the rise of Fascism created the same sense of a minority embattled in defence of truth against the force of national self-deception, portrays the confident innocence of the 'Dreyfusards of the first hour'. They had evidence that the mole in the French military intelligence was not Dreyfus but one Major Esterhazy, and did not imagine that what they saw as the truth would be subordinated to the corporate interest of the army and to raison d'état.

With such a collection of documents and facts no trace of doubt remained in our minds. Our certainty was pure, whole and serious, and we were convinced that it would be shared spontaneously by the whole universe, once the universe was informed of what we had learned ourselves. This illusion must seem extraordinary today, after everything that happened, but it should seem natural if people try to put themselves in our place. The Dreyfusards have been accused of engineering a treacherous plot to divide France and tear it apart. But they did not and I think could not have suspected that there would be a Dreyfus Affair. For them everything was clear, luminous, obvious, and they did not doubt that universal reason must be persuaded by this truth. For the moment, at the end of the holidays [of 1897] public opinion was calm and indifferent; it was unaware and expected nothing. Yet when the truth was revealed what a generous cry would be heard throughout France! The nation had abhorred the crime as one, and as one it would proclaim the error and set it right! Three years before, people had wondered what punishments could chastise the traitor enough; now they would wonder what praises and rewards would even begin to rehabilitate the victim. Those who had had the misfortune to be closest concerned in the fateful proceedings, the judges of Dreyfus, his friends, his commanding officers, would be the first to make their confession and to express their remorse. We were enchanted by that prospect. The only painful, anxious feeling we had was one of impatience. For until he returned to France to be showered with flowers and good wishes, to be consoled by the commiseration of a whole country, the innocent was still far away, in chains on his torrid rock. He would be freed when the truth was made public, but when would that be? When would be the chosen moment? Feverishly we counted the days.

Léon Blum, *Souvenirs sur l'Affaire*, Gallimard, 1935, pp. 41–3.

DOCUMENT 12   J'ACCUSE

Émile Zola's intervention was provoked by the clearing of Esterhazy by a military court, which left Dreyfus as guilty as ever. Zola's letter to the President of the Republic, published on 13 January 1898, is an indictment of military justice, the military hierarchy and the military mind, and alludes to the threat of a military coup d'état. It betrays the same faith in the inevitable triumph of truth as the previous extract by Blum did.

How could one military court be expected to overrule what another military court had done?

I am not even talking about the possible choice of judges. Isn't the higher notion of discipline which runs in the veins of these soldiers enough to invalidate their powers of equity? Discipline entails obedience. Do you expect a military court formally to contradict a minister of war, the great leader, when he has publicly proclaimed the finality of the court's decision to the applause of parliament? From a hierarchical point of view it is impossible.

An iniquitous verdict was returned [the acquittal of Esterhazy] which will always hang heavy on our military courts and cast a veil of suspicion over all their decisions. The first court [which condemned Dreyfus] might have been unintelligent, but the second [which acquitted Esterhazy] was necessarily criminal. Its excuse, I repeat, is that the supreme chief had spoken, proclaiming the verdict to be indefeasible, holy and above men, in such a way that no inferiors could contradict it. We are told about the honour of the army, and the need to love and respect it. Certainly, we have nothing but love and respect for the army which marches out at the first sign of danger, which would defend French soil, which is the whole people. But we are talking about another sort of army, upon whose dignity we are calling in our demand for justice. That army is the sabre, the dictator who may be forced upon us tomorrow. And God knows that I will not piously kiss the hilt of a sabre!

[There follows a series of accusations levelled against named officers of the military, from the Minister of War, General Mercier, downwards.] I do not know the people I am accusing, I have never seen them and I bear them neither bitterness nor hatred. For me they are only entities, spirits of evil-doing in society. My act today is nothing but a revolutionary means of hastening the explosion of justice and truth.

Emile Zola, *La Vérité en Marche*, Paris 1901, pp. 36–7, 93.

DOCUMENT 13 THE DREYFUS AFFAIR SEEN BY NATIONALISTS

This extract is from a letter from the French commander at Fashoda, Marchand, to the cartoonist Forain. Forain had pictured him pensive under a tricolor, while in the foreground Kitchener was saying to a clergyman, 'How can I demoralise this good man?' and the reply came, 'I will have a go by reading him a few French papers.' Marchand had seen this cartoon in a newspaper given to him by the British. The message was that the campaign of the Dreyfusards – the enemy within – undermined the morale of the army and in the end made it unwilling to defend a fatherland which had sunk to such depths.

It was the 21 September, at Fashoda. For nearly ten months we had had no news from France or Europe. Forty-eight hours previously the Anglo-Egyptian army had arrived at Omdurman and the Sirdar Kitchener was going to return to Khartoum.

On the orders of his commander and doubtless with honourable intentions, Wingate left me a collection of English newspapers and some French ones, *for which we had not dared ask*, but which we accepted with gratitude ...

I have only two lines to add. An hour after opening the French papers the ten officers were shaking and crying. We learned that the terrible Dreyfus

Affair had been reopened by the horrible campaign of those vile people. For thirty-six hours we were incapable of saying anything to each other. Such feelings cannot be shared.

I have enlarged, exaggerated or changed nothing. On the contrary.

I just want to tell you as I look at the last Forain cartoon of October [1898] which has travelled 3,000 miles to get here, that you must have a deep sense of proud patriotism. Otherwise you could not draw as you do.

For that reason I ask permission to embrace you, if you will permit me.

Major Marchand

Maurice Barrès, *Scènes et Doctrines du Nationalisme*, Paris, 1902, pp. 371–2.

DOCUMENT 14   **FACES OF RADICALISM**

These two extracts illustrate the difference between the claims and the actual policies of the Radical party. Document (a) is an exposition by Camille Pelletan of a broad agenda of reforms at the founding congress of the Republican, Radical and Radical-Socialist Party. Document (b) is an interpellation of the Combes government by Alexandre Millerand. He was chairman of a commission on social insurance, but was unable to obtain the support of the government for a pensions bill, partly because of the costs involved, partly because of its obsession with destroying the power of the Church.

(a) The first thought of the republican congress should be one of union against the common enemy. That thought must be the concern of all democrats defending themselves against open plots and schemes of *coup d'état.*

That thought has brought us together here though it extends far beyond these walls, for it rallies all the sons of the Revolution, whatever their differences, against all partisans of counter-revolution, their numbers swollen by accomplices found in the ranks of our erstwhile friends.

The best way to defend the Republic is to make it more republican ... Most of the reforms promised still await enactment. Their time should have come long ago, and we can delay no longer. First come the reforms concerning clericalism. The law against teaching congregations is on the statute book. The country expects it to be enforced without weakness. If necessary it will require it. The struggle is on, and we must fight to the end ... No one can consider the pact forged against liberty between the Papacy and the renascent Napoleonic dictatorship to be a republican institution. However we should not air our differences on this until the time has come to dissolve it: universal suffrage will decide.

Another danger is growing daily in all countries. That is the power that the concentration and handling of large capital is giving to high finance. We must protect the general interest of the country and the liberty and prosperity of all from its growing domination both by legislation against speculation and laws to nationalise certain monopolies and public services as the interests of national defence and agricultural and industrial production demand it.

Among the most pressing concerns in modern societies are social reforms. What divides us from the socialists is our passionate commitment to the principle of private property, the abolition of which we cannot even begin to contemplate. But precisely because this principle rests entirely on the inviolable right of each person to the fruit of his labour, we will defer to no one when it comes to introducing old-age pensions in a practicable way, to preventing large-scale industry from becoming a new feudalism, and to speeding up the peaceful process which will make workers owners of their tools and ensure the just remuneration of their labour.

Fiscal reforms are no less urgent. Our tax system weighs lightly on the rich and heavily on the poor, especially on the mass of peasants who form the majority and the strength of the country. We desire a progressive income tax which will lighten the burden on workers and particularly on villages. We want a general overhaul of the old system, especially a reform of the land tax and taxes which tie up rural property.

Add to this equality of military service, reduced to two years.

That is the outline of our programme.

A declaration of Radical principles and policies by Camille Pelletan at the founding congress of 1901, cited by Jean-Thomas Nordmann, *La France Radicale*, 'Archives', Gallimard Julliard, Paris, 1977, pp. 44–6.

(**b**) I come to this desk to demand an explanation from the president of the council – and this is something which concerns the general policy of the government to the highest degree – of an attitude which is in formal contradiction with the promises made by the cabinet and which is preventing the commission [on social insurance] from making any headway.

... I could never have imagined that any government could limit the horizon of its ambitions to the struggle against the religious congregations. ('*Hear, hear!' on several benches on the left and centre.*)

What assures a place apart in the history of the republican party and the gratitude of the people for the author of the law of 1901 [Waldeck-Rousseau] is that he is also the author of the law of 1884 [on trade-union rights] and that at no time, even at the most critical moments, did he as head of the government of 1899 separate social policy from republican defence.

In fact the sharper the struggle with the forces of the past, the heavier the obligation on republican government to give the same drive and passion to building the new world so impatiently awaited as it does to the necessary task of pulling down the old one.

No one is more conscious than I of the fearful difficulties posed by a pensions bill. But precisely because the task is difficult and complex the republican party must pursue it with a tireless resolution, without being distracted from its goal. It will be assured that far from weakening it, this fight for justice and the improvement of the lot of the workers will give the party incomparable strength and credit in its daily battle with the enemies of the Republic, whether they show their faces or not.

Alexandre Millerand in the Chamber of Deputies, 17 March 1904, *Journal Officiel. Débats parlementaires. Chambre des Députés*, January–March 1904, p. 786.

DOCUMENT 15   **REVOLUTION AS MYTH AND REALITY**

The Radical party was committed to the ideology of Revolution, but felt rather differently when public order was at stake. The death of a demonstrator during the Seine labourers' strike of 1908 provoked a massive political crisis which exposed the paradoxes of the Radical position. In document (a), Clemenceau, the President of the Council of Ministers, defends the policy of his government in the Chamber of Deputies against attack from the Left. In document (b), Jaurès continues the attack in the socialist daily, L'Humanité.

(a) M. THE PRESIDENT OF THE COUNCIL [Clemenceau]: You said that I was the enemy of socialism and of the working class. I reply: you do not represent socialism or the working class. I am a French citizen placed by chance in a difficult position ... the responsibility of which I feel more keenly than others, as I should. You thought that you could frighten the government with verbal and physical violence. Well, the government is not frightened. (*Applause on the left and centre.*) That is its crime! It is not your enemy; it is not the workers' enemy and I have said as much. Its only enemies are those who break the law ...

M. PAUL CONSTANS: Like the gendarmes.

M. THE PRESIDENT OF THE COUNCIL: because it has to ensure that the law is observed ...

You will never find a government which allows anarchy to take a hold in this country, smashing cars, clubbing people, throwing stones at miners at work in the pit.

M. JAURÈS: You are anarchy crowned. (*'Hear, hear!' on the extreme left.*)

M. THE PRESIDENT OF THE COUNCIL: Fine. A nice piece of rhetoric.

I am anarchist because I enforce the right to work. I am anarchist because I won't tolerate navvies being thrown into the Seine. I am anarchist because I won't permit houses to be set on fire. I am anarchist because I won't allow people to be beaten up with clubs. That is where we differ.

You see that in this motion something quite other than the Draveil-Vigneux incident is at stake ... a dead body is being exploited to attack the government and you say that we are responsible for this policy ...

M. EDOUARD VAILLANT: It's your policy which puts guns into the hands of gendarmes.

M. THE PRESIDENT OF THE COUNCIL: Messieurs, I have finished. The government cannot be held in the least responsible for events it is the first to deplore (*Exclamations on the extreme left*), as I said to begin with.

Such things have happened under all governments, they are unavoidable. Our duty is the same as that of all previous governments – to uphold justice – and that we shall do.

The House will declare whether it condemns this anarchy, or whether it thinks that for the good of the future social revolution we must grapple with revolutionaries who want only disorder and violence. It will declare whether it wants to help us establish a legal order which opens the way to reform in order to prevent revolution. That is the policy that the government is proposing. (*Loud applause on a large number of benches.*)

Speech of Clemenceau in the Chamber of Deputies, 11 June 1908. *Journal Officiel. Débats parlementaires. Chambre des Députés*, January–July 1908, pp. 1166–7.

(b) M. Clemenceau made a moving case for the murderous gendarmes of Draveil, and the Chamber gave him authority to use the appropriate repressive measures ... M. Clemenceau declared that we alone were responsible and alone ought to be court-martialled. The murderers will be summoned only to be congratulated, because they have fought the good fight against 'the Revolution' denounced yesterday by M. Clemenceau. This evocation of the revolutionary peril by all governments as they slide inevitably towards reaction is a miserable comedy. Méline performed it, [Casimir-] Périer too, perhaps with less vulgarity than the current president of the council. Those Radicals who have now decided to follow conservative policies to the bitter end were right yesterday to support M. Clemenceau ... Socialism will be isolated, exposed to many attacks, and buffeted by winds from every horizon. But democracy, which seems to have lost its way, will one day advance to meet it.

A massive conservative coalition is now forming against us, against the proletariat. M. Clemenceau has never been other than a negative force and was predestined to this negative action. He succeeded in upsetting the republican and democratic victory of 1906. But he will not break the strength of the working class and socialism. They will organise with an energy renewed by the trials they have endured, and with a force and faith only increased by the universal unleashing of blind hatred.

Article by Jean Jaurès in *L'Humanité*, 12 June 1908.

DOCUMENT 16   **WAR AND REVOLUTION**

The Paris Commune was as much patriotic as revolutionary. Here the military governor of Paris, General Trochu, describes the series of coups *against the incompetent provisional government which culminated in the insurrection of 18 March 1871. Trochu was removed from his post in an attempt to placate the angry Parisians after the defeat of Buzenval on 19 January 1871, but to no avail.*

I have placed before you a sort of history of the Paris sectarians during the siege. I have demonstrated that each of their assaults on public order coincided with one of our [military] disasters, as if they wanted to complete them and exploit them: on 8 October, after the surrender of Strasbourg; on 31 October, after the surrender of Metz; on 22 January, after the battle of Buzenval ... All the assaults were planned and executed in a spirit of violence: hatred of the government and a feeling that the Government of National Defence was betraying the country because it did not order a mass mobilisation. They demanded war to the death and insisted that they would have it, with or without the government. In the same spirit they seized the cannon which had been placed on the Place de Wagram and carried them to Montmartre, where the bastion of the insurrection was erected.

Testimony of General Trochu to the National Assembly, 15 June 1871, *Journal Officiel*, 16 June 1871, p. 1379.

DOCUMENT 17   **WHAT IS A NATION?**

The lecture by Ernest Renan, given at the Sorbonne in 1882, and entitled What is a Nation? *rejects theories that the nation is based on race, language or religion and argues that it is based on collective memory and collective will. While it has become a classic statement of the view that nations are constructed by collective will rather than determined by ethnic realities, beloved by theorists of nationalism, it can still be read as a tract for the times, seeking to draw some positive lessons from the defeat of 1870 and holding out some hope for the recovery of Alsace-Lorraine.*

The nation is a soul, a spiritual principle. Two elements which, in truth, are but one, constitute this soul, this spiritual principle. One is the past, the other is the present. One is the common ownership of a common heritage of memories, the other is present agreement, the desire to live together, the will to continue to build on an inheritance that has been received undivided. Man, sirs, does not improvise. The nation, like the individual, is the end product of a lengthy past of work, sacrifice and devotion. The worship of ancestors is the most legitimate of cults, since our ancestors have made us what we are. A heroic past, great men, glory (by which I mean the genuine article) is the social capital on which the national idea is based. To have common glories in the past, a common will in the present, to have accomplished great things together, to wish to do so again, that is the essential condition for being a nation. We love in proportion to the sacrifices we have agreed to and to the pain we have suffered. We love the house we have built and pass on. The Spartan song, 'We are what you were, we shall be what you are' is in its simplicity the national anthem of every country.

In the past, a heritage of glory and sadness to share, a common programme to realise in the future; to have suffered, celebrated, hoped together, that is worth far more than free-trade areas and frontiers meeting strategic requirements. That can be understood, in spite of differences of race and language. I said 'to have suffered together'; indeed, collective suffering unites more than joy. Mourning is more important for national memory than victory, for it imposes obligations, it demands a collective effort.

A nation is thus a great solidarity, constituted by the sense of sacrifices that people have made and others that they are yet ready to make. It supposes a past, but it is summed up in the present by a tangible fact: the agreement, the desire clearly expressed, to continue collective life. The existence of a nation is (if you will pardon this expression) an everyday plebiscite, just as the existence of the individual is a perpetual affirmation of life. Oh! I know, it is less metaphysical than divine right, less brutal than some pretended historical claim. In the scheme of ideas that I submit to you, a nation has more right than a king to say to a province, 'You belong to me, I am taking you'. A province, in our opinion, is its inhabitants. If someone has the right to be consulted in this matter, it is the inhabitant. A nation never has a real interest in annexing or holding onto a country against its will. In conclusion, the will of nations is the only criterion, and that to which we must always return.

Renan, 'Qu'est-ce qu'une Nation?' *Oeuvres complètes I*, Calmann-Lévy, Paris, 1947, pp. 903–5.

DOCUMENT 18   TWO VIEWS OF COLONIALISM

France's colonial policy was controversial. For some it represented the prospect of recovering some form of national greatness without antagonizing Germany. For others the very supine position before Germany which that strategy entailed was enough to condemn it. The question was made more bitter by party-political disputes. Colonies were initially the policy of the Opportunist republicans, particularly of Jules Ferry, whose praises are sung in document (a) by Charles de Freycinet (whose work was first published in 1913). But colonial adventures were disliked by the Radicals, often supported by the Right. In document (b) Clemenceau voices his hostility to the Tonkin expedition in a debate which finished off the Ferry ministry.

(a) M. Jules Ferry must be congratulated for understanding how much France suffered from the loss of its colonial empire. The acquisition of Algeria and even of Tunisia did not end the regrets caused by the loss of so many glorious possessions in Asia and Africa in the eighteenth century. These regrets had become even sharper after the disastrous war of 1871. France felt diminished both in territory and in glory. Direct revenge was impossible, but she wanted at least to deploy her armed forces, to show that they were still strong. Compensation could not be found close by, so it was sought far off. Inevitably she was going to move into other parts of the world, imitating in this respect most of the other great European nations. M. Jules Ferry appreciated this mentality and, without positively planning the founding of a colonial empire, he exploited opportunities which arose to achieve it. The enterprise was not illusory, and the shock waves are still being felt. The Asian epic was followed by the African epic. After Annam and Tonkin France directed her energies to the Sudan, the Congo and Dahomey. As if these territories were not enough to absorb her energies, France is today staking a claim to Morocco, in spite of difficulties, even dangers, of which she is not unaware. Though mistakes have been made, M. Jules Ferry has the good fortune to remain the initiator of our twentieth-century colonial expansion.

Charles de Freycinet, *Souvenirs, 1878–1893*, Da Capo Press, New York, 1973, pp. 268–9.

(b) Messieurs, Prince Bismarck is a dangerous enemy; he is perhaps even more dangerous as a friend. Yes! it was he who dangled Tunis in front of you at the Congress of Berlin; he who put you at loggerheads with England as I said just now; he who is negotiating with you about the Congo at the conference table of Berlin. And while we are wasting our money and the best of our blood in crazy enterprises, he is waging a terrible economic war against us, and patiently awaiting his fee for services rendered.

If I establish that there is an immediate, pressing interest not only from the financial point of view, but also from the point of view of our policy in Europe, concerning what remains and can remain of our dignity among the countries of Europe; if I can establish that there is still time to change our policy, that we can stop these colonial expeditions which take our gold and the best of our blood by killing the flower of our army, then you must take a decision which involves much more than the Tonkin expedition.

I know full well that we will take Tonkin. I know that our gallant soldiers will defeat the Chinese wherever they confront them. I don't doubt it, and no one ever has doubted it. But the question at the moment is not Tonkin but something higher. The question is France. (*Loud applause on the extreme left and right.*)

Speech of Clemenceau to the Chamber of Deputies, in *Journal Officiel. Débats parlementaires. Chambre des Députés*, 28 November 1884, p. 1501.

DOCUMENT 19   CAN A REPUBLIC BE GREAT?

For the royalist Charles Maurras, Republic and greatness were mutually exclusive terms. In this piece, written in the aftermath of Fashoda and the Dreyfus Affair, Maurras turns for evidence to the reflections of Ernest Renan after 1870, and takes a few liberties with French history. Maurras died in 1952.

Renan wrote these words: 'The day France cut her king's head off, she committed suicide.'

Louis XIV bequeathed France an army and a navy. The restoration [of 1815] left her a magnificent position in Europe. Louis-Philippe left the military organisation created by the law of 1832, by which I mean the troops who won the Crimean War. Such was the work of the House of France in its last moments. The dynasty succumbed and from that time we have been falling. Catastrophes unknown since the fifteenth century (except that in the fifteenth century the national dynasty pulled itself together and the country with it) have repeatedly exhausted us. What are Pavia and Rossbach, so often mentioned, when compared to Sedan and Waterloo? Revolutions have succeeded revolutions. The state is bankrupt. Three times foreigners have invaded Paris. We have had two civil wars. We have witnessed Italian unification, German unification, and the outrageous growth of the double Anglo-Saxon Empire.

Never has political France been so small. Since then she has achieved a masterpiece of littleness: she has made herself a Republic, which means she has decided to be weak and defeated. Renan warned us about it. 'There are some,' he said, 'who imagine a powerful, influential, glorious Republic. Let them think again and choose. Of course the Republic is possible in France, but a Republic scarcely more important than the Swiss Republic – and less respected. The Republic can have neither army nor diplomacy; the Republic would be a singularly useless military state, with extremely poor discipline. The basis of a Republic is election, and a republican society is as weak as a military unit which elects its officers. The fear of not being re-elected paralyses all energy.'

Energy. Our deputies may well show some for an immediate interest, which arrests the eye, which the crowd sees and applauds. They have no energy for a future interest, however grave it might be. They reckon with 1902 and 1906 [dates of elections], but not with 1950. 1950 could not be further from their thoughts. Living Frenchmen with the vote are their only concern.

What this country is lacking is an instrument of foresight in the central government. What it lacks, to be truthful, is a future.

Charles Maurras, *Une Campagne royaliste au 'Figaro', 1901–2*, Nouvelle Imprimerie Nationale, 1925, pp. 496–7.

DOCUMENT 20 SOCIALISM AND REVOLUTION

The achievement of Jaurès was to reconcile the commitment of the French working class to the cause of international socialism and a commitment to the defence of the fatherland. This he did by reference to the revolutionary-patriotic tradition of 1792, in which France, the patrie, *or land of liberty, was defended by volunteer forces against Austrian and Prussian armies. These volunteers then went on to liberate oppressed peoples. The defence of France was thus equated with the defence of liberty and civilization on behalf of humanity. This is the burden of the speech of the trade-union leader, Jouhaux, at the graveside of the murdered Jaurès in 1914.*

Jaurès consoled us in our passionate drive for peace. It is neither his fault nor ours if peace has not prevailed. Before we march off to the great massacre, in the name of those workers who have already left, in the name of those who are about to leave, including myself, I proclaim before this coffin our hatred of the imperialism and savage militarism which have unleashed this horrible crime.

... If he were still here, if a cowardly assassin had not stifled his voice for ever, he would tell us, comrades, that you will be defending not just the national cause but the cause of the International and that of civilisation, the cradle of which is France.

... Caught up in the struggle, we will rise to repel the invader, to safeguard the patrimony of civilisation and generous ideology bequeathed to us by history. We do not wish those few liberties we snatched with such difficulty from evil forces to be lost. Our wish has always been to enlarge popular rights, and to widen the field of liberties. It is because of this wish that we answer 'present' to the mobilisation order. We will never fight a war of conquest.

... The working class remembers that it has always been nourished by revolutionary traditions of the soldiers of the Year II who took liberty to the world, that it must not arm in hatred of a people and that it must not direct its anger against a nation which is itself a victim of despots and bad leaders.

Emperors of Germany and Austria-Hungary, Prussian Junkers and great Austrian lords who have sought war out of hatred for democracy, we swear to ring the knell of your regimes.

We will be the soldiers of liberty who create freedom for the oppressed and harmony between nations through mutual understanding and an alliance of peoples. With this ideal we will conquer.

Yes, Jaurès, your everlasting memory will guide us in the terrible conflict which is beginning. It will stand before us like a flame that the torment will not extinguish. And before I go to meet the danger, I will proclaim aloud our indestructible faith in the International, and our resolution to secure every liberty by bitter struggle for those who await them in hope.

No, comrades, our ideal of human reconciliation and happiness in society will not fade. It has been checked, but even so better conditions to spread it around the world are being prepared.

The shadow of the great Jaurès bears witness to this.

Speech of Léon Jouhaux at the funeral of Jean Jaurès, 4 August 1914, in Jean Rabaut, *L'Antimilitarisme français*, Paris, 1975, pp. 104–7.

BIBLIOGRAPHY

WHICH REPUBLIC?

General accounts

1   Anderson, R., *France, 1870–1914*, Routledge and Kegan Paul, 1977.
2   Wright, G., *France in Modern Times*, Murray, 3rd edition, 1981.
3   Mayeur, J. M. and Rebérioux, M., *The Third Republic from its Origins to 1914*, Cambridge University Press, 1984. This is a translation of *Les Débuts de la Troisième République*, Seuil, 1973 and *La République radicale?*, Seuil, 1975.
4   Agulhon, M., *The French Republic, 1879–1992*, Blackwell, Oxford, 1993.
5   Zeldin, T., *France, 1848–1945*, 2 vols. Oxford University Press, Oxford, 1973 and 1977.
6   Rosanvallon, P., *Le Sacre du Citoyen. Histoire du Suffrage universel en France*, Gallimard, Paris, 1992.

The foundation of the Republic

7   Greenberg, L. M., *Sisters of Liberty. Marseille, Lyon, Paris and the Reaction to the Centralized State, 1868–1871*, Harvard University Press, Harvard, 1971
8   Howard, M., *The Franco-Prussian War*, Rupert Hart-Davis, 1968.
9   Bury, J. P. T., *Gambetta and the National Defence*, Longman, 1936.
10   Bury, J. P. T. and Tombs, R., *Thiers, 1797–1877. A Political Biography*, Allen and Unwin, 1986.
11   Société d'Histoire de la Révolution de 1848 et des Révolutions du XIXe siècle, *Blanqui et les Blanquistes* SEDES, 1986.
12   Tombs, R., *The War against Paris, 1871*, Cambridge University Press, Cambridge, 1981.
13   de Mun, A., *Ma Vocation Sociale,* P. Lethielleux, Paris, 1908.
14   Osgood, S., *French Royalism since 1870*, Martinus Nijhoff, The Hague, 1970.
15   Locke, R., *French Legitimists and the Politics of Moral Order in the Early Third Republic*, Princeton University Press, 1974.

16   Bury, J. P. T., *Gambetta and the Making of the Third Republic*,
      Longman, 1973.
17   Wartelle, J-C., 'L'Élection Barodet, avril 1873', *Revue d'Histoire
      Moderne et Contemporaine*, pp. 600–30, 1980.
18   Rothney, J., *Bonapartism after Sedan*, Cornell University Press, 1978.
19   Bertocci, P. A., *Jules Simon. Republican Anticlericalism and Cultural
      Politics in France, 1848–1886*, University of Missouri Press, 1978.
20   Agulhon, M., *Marianne into Battle. Republican Imagery and
      Symbolism in France*, Cambridge University Press, Cambridge,
      1981.
21   Rudelle, O., *La République Absolue. Aux origines de l'instabilité
      ministérielle de la France contemporaine, 1870–1889*, Sorbonne,
      1982.

THE REPUBLIC OF THE NOTABLES

22   Derfler, L., *President and Parliament. A Short History of the French
      Presidency*, Florida University Press, 1983.
23   Bury, J. P. T., *Gambetta's Final Years, 1877–1882*, Longman, 1982.
24   Estèbe, J., *Les Ministres de la République, 1871–1914*, Fondation
      Nationale des Sciences Politiques, 1982.
25   Salem, D., 'Le Sénat "conservateur" de la Troisième République',
      Revue d'Histoire Économique et Sociale, 50, pp. 518–50, 1972.
26   Dogan, M., 'Les Filières de la carrière politique en France', *Revue
      française de Sociologie*, 8, pp. 468–92, 1967.
27   Dogan, M., 'La Stabilité du personnel parlementaire sous la
      Troisième République', *Revue française de Science Politique*, 3,
      pp. 319–348, 1953.
28   Guiral, P. and Thuillier, G., *La Vie Quotidienne des Députés en
      France de 1871 à 1914*, Hachette, 1980.
29   de Jouvenel, R., *La République des Camarades*, First edn 1914,
      Grasset, p. 17, 1934.
30   Pilenco, A., *Les Mœurs du Suffrage Universel en France, 1848–1928*,
      Revue Mondiale, 1930.
31   Goujon, P., *Le Vigneron Citoyen. Mâconnais et Chalonnais,
      1848–1914*, CTHS, 1993.
32   Gildea, R., *Education in Provincial France. A Study of Three
      Departments*, Clarendon Press, Oxford, 1983.

LEFT AND RIGHT

33   Bidelman, P. K., *Pariahs stand up! The Founding of the Liberal
      Feminist Movement in France, 1858–1889*, Westport, Connecticut,
      1982.
34   Duroselle, J-B., *Clemenceau*, Fayard, 1988.

35   Gaillard, J-M., *Jules Ferry*, Fayard, 1989.
36   Joughin, J. T., *The Paris Commune and French Politics, 1871–1880*, Johns Hopkins University Press, 1955.
37   Elwitt, S., *The Making of the Third Republic. Class and Politics in France, 1868–1884*, Louisiana State University Press, 1975.
38   Smith, M. S., 'Free trade and protection in the early Third Republic', *French Historical Studies*, 10, pp. 293–314, 1977.
39   Ageron, C-R., *L'Anticolonialisme en France de 1871 à 1914*, Presses Universitaires de France, 1973.
40   Rutkoff, P., *Revanche and Revision. The Ligue des Patriotes and the Origin of the Political Right in France, 1882–1900*, Ohio University Press, 1981.
41   Sirinelli, J-F., *Histoire des Droites en France*, Gallimard, Paris, 1992, I. *La Politique* Ch. III. 1.
42   Martin, B., *Count Albert de Mun, Paladin of the Third Republic*, Chapel Hill, University of North Carolina, 1978.
43   el Gammal, J., 'Un Pré-Ralliement: Raoul-Duval et la Droite républicaine, 1885–1887', *Revue d'Histoire Moderne et Contemporaine*, 29, pp. 599–621, 1982.
44   Dansette, A., *L'Affaire Wilson et la Chute du Président Grévy*, Perrin, 1936.
45   Seager, F. H., *The Boulanger Affair*, Cornell University Press, 1969.
46   Mermeix (Gabriel Terrail), *Les Coulisses du Boulangisme*, Cerf, 1890.
47   Néré, J., 'Les Elections de Boulanger dans le département du Nord', complementary thesis, Paris, 1959.
48   Burns, M., *Rural society and French politics. Boulangism and the Dreyfus Affair, 1886–1900*, Princeton University Press, 1984.
49   de Freycinet, C., *Souvenirs 1878–1893*, De Capo Press, New York, 1973.
50   Irvine, W. D., *The Boulanger Affair Reconsidered. Royalism, Boulangism and the Origins of the Radical Right in France*, Oxford University Press, Oxford, 1988.

SOCIAL STRUCTURE

51   Moulin, A., *Peasantry and Society in France since 1789*, Cambridge University Press/Maison des Sciences de l'Homme, 1991, Ch. 3.
52   Levine Frader, L., *Peasants and Protest. Agricultural Workers, Politics and Unions in the Aude, 1850–1914*, University of California Press, 1991.
53   Weber, E., *Peasants into Frenchmen. The Modernization of Rural France, 1870–1914*, Chatto and Windus, 1977.
54   Duby G. and Wallon A., eds, *Histoire de la France rurale*, vol. 3, Seuil, 1976.

55   Loubere, L., *The Red and the White*, Albany, 1978.
56   Gratton, P., *La Lutte des Classes dans les Campagnes*, Editions Anthropos, 1971.
57   Guillaumin, E., *Six Ans de Lutte Syndicale*, Editions de Cahiers Bourbonnais, Moulins, 1977.
58   Berger, S., *Peasants against Politics. Rural Organization in Brittany, 1911–1967*, Harvard University Press, 1972.
59   Lequin, Y., 'Labour in the French Economy since the Revolution', *Cambridge Economic History*, VII, Cambridge University Press, Cambridge, 1978.
60   Noiriel, G., *Workers in French Society in the Nineteenth and Twentieth Centuries*, Berg, 1990, Chs. 2 and 3.
61   Jonas, R. A., *Industry and Politics in Rural France. Peasants of the Isère, 1870–1914*, Cornell University Press, 1994.
62   Magraw, R., *A History of the French Working Class* vol. II. *Workers and the Bourgeois Republic*, Blackwell, Oxford, 1992, part V.
63   Hanagan, M. P., *The Logic of Solidarity. Artisans and Industrial Workers in Three French Towns*, University of Illinois Press, 1980.
64   Hilden, P., *Working Women and Socialist Politics in France, 1880–1914. A Regional Study*, Clarendon Press, Oxford, 1986.
65   Accampo, E., *Industrialization, Family Life and Class Relations. Saint-Chamond, 1815–1914*, University of California Press, 1989.
66   Perrot, M., *Workers on Strike. France 1871–1890*, Berg, 1987.
67   Ridley, F. F., *Revolutionary Syndicalism in France*, Cambridge University Press, Cambridge, 1970.
68   Jennings, J., 'The CGT and the Couriau Affair: syndicalist responses to female labour in France before 1914', *European History Quarterly*, 21, pp. 321–37, 1991.
69   Michel, J., 'Syndicalisme minier et politique dans Nord/Pas-de-Calais: le cas Basly, 1880–1914', *Le Mouvement Social*, 87, pp. 9–33, 1974.
70   Schöttler, P., *Naissance des Bourses du Travail*, Presses Universitaires de France, 1985.
71   Baudelot, C., Establet, R., Malemort, J., *La Petite Bourgeoisie en France*, Maspéro, 1974.
72   Raison-Jourde, F., *La Colonie auvergnate de Paris au XIXe siècle*, Commission des Travaux Historiques, Paris, 1976.
73   Faure, A., 'L'Épicerie parisienne au XIXe siècle ou la corporation éclatée', *Le Mouvement Social*, 108, pp. 113–30, 1979.
74   Wishnia, J., *The Proletaranizing of the Fonctionnaires. Civil Service Workers and the Labour Movement under the Third Republic*, Louisiana State University Press, 1992.
75   Offen, K., 'The Second Sex and the baccalauréat in republican France, 1880–1924' *French Historical Studies*, 13, pp. 252–86, 1983.

76 Weisz, G., *The Emergence of Modern Universities in France, 1863–1914*, Princeton University Press, 1983.

77 Lévy-Leboyer, M., 'Le Patronat français a-t-il été malthusien?' *Le Mouvement Social*, 88, pp. 3–49, 1974.

78 Lévy-Leboyer, M., 'The large corporation in France', in A. D. Chandler and H. Daems eds, *Managerial Hierarchies*, Harvard University Press, 1980.

79 Daumard, A., *Les Bourgeois et les Bourgeoisies en France depuis 1815*, Flammarion, 1991.

80 Charle, C., *Les Hauts Fonctionnaires en France au XIXe siècle*, 'Archives', Gallimard Julliard, 1986.

81 Charle, C., *Les Élites de la République, 1880–1900*, Fayard, 1987.

82 Charle, C., *A Social History of France in the Nineteenth Century*, Berg, 1994.

SOCIALISM

83 Rebérioux, M., 'Le Socialisme français', in J. Droz ed., *Histoire générale du Socialisme*, Presses Universitaires de France, 1974.

84 Bergounioux, A., 'Socialisme et République avant 1914' in Serge Berstein and Odile Rudelle eds., *Le Modèle républicain*, PUF, 1992.

85 Willard, C., *Le Mouvement socialiste en France, 1893–1905: les Guesdistes*, Editions Sociales, 1965.

86 Stuart, R., *Marxism at Work. Ideology, Class and French Socialism during the Third Republic*, Cambridge University Press, Cambridge, 1992.

87 Stafford, D., *From Anarchism to Reformism*, Weidenfeld and Nicholson, 1971.

88 Baker, R. P., 'Socialism in the Nord, 1880–1914', *International Review of Social History*, 12, pp. 357–89, 1967

89 Charnay, M., *Les Allemanists*, M. Rivière, 1912, p. 45.

90 Winock, M., 'La scission de Châtellerault et la naissance du Parti allemaniste', *Le Mouvement Social*, 75, pp. 33–62, 1971.

91 Julliard, *Fernand Pelloutier et les Origines du Syndicalisme d'Action Directe*, Seuil, 1971.

92 Rebérioux, 'Le Mur des Fédérés', in Pierre Nora, *Les Lieux de Mémoire. I. La République*, Gallimard. Nouvelle Revue Française, pp. 619–49, 1984.

93 Hutton, P., *The Cult of the Revolutionary Tradition: the Blanquists in French Politics, 1864–1893*, University of California Press, 1981.

94 Vincent, K. S., *Between Marxism and Anarchism: Benoît Malon and French Reformist Socialism*, University of California Press, 1992.

95 Rebérioux, M., ed., *Fourmies et les Premier Mai*, Atelier, 1994.

96 Derfler, L., *Paul Lafargue and the Founding of French Marxism, 1842–1882*, Harvard University Press, 1991.

97   Derfler, L., *Alexandre Millerand. The Socialist Years*, Mouton, Paris
      – The Hague, 1977.
98   Milbank Farrar, M., *Principled Pragmatist, The Political Career of
      Alexandre Millerand*, Berg, 1991.
99   Trempé, R., *Les Mineurs de Carmaux, 1848–1914*, 2 vols, Éditions
      Ouvrières, 1971.
100   Goldberg, H., *Life of Jean Jaurès*, University of Wisconsin Press,
      1962.
101   Berlanstein, L., *The Working People of Paris, 1871–1914*, Johns
      Hopkins University Press, 1984.
102   Landauer, C., 'The Origins of socialist Reformism in France',
      International Review of Social History, 12, pp. 81–107, 1967.
103   Derruo-Boniol, 'Le Socialisme dans l'Allier de 1848 à 1914', *Cahiers
      d'Histoire*, 2, pp. 115–61, 1957.
104   Judt, T., *Socialism in Provence, 1871–1914*, Cambridge University
      Press, 1979, argues instead that the adoption of socialism by the
      peasants of the Var represented a break with the past and with the
      Radical middle class.
105   de Goustine, C., *Pouget, Les Matins noirs du Syndicalisme*, Édition
      de la Tête de Feuilles, Paris, 1971.
106   Joll, J., *The Anarchists*, Eyre and Spottiswoode, 1964, 2nd ed., 1979.
107   Maitron, J., *Le Mouvement anarchiste en France*, I, Maspéro, 1975.
108   Pelloutier, F., 'L'Anarchisme et les syndicats ouvriers', *Les Temps
      nouveaux*, 2–8 November 1895.
109   Maitron, J., *Paul Delesalle. Un Anarchiste de la Belle Époque*,
      Fayard, 1985.

THE CONSOLIDATION OF THE ELITE

110   Smith, M. S., *Tariff Reform in France, 1860–1900. The Politics of
      Economic Interest*, Cornell University Press, 1980.
111   Lebovics, H., *The Alliance of Iron and Wheat in the Third French
      Republic, 1860–1914. Origins of the New Conservatism*, Louisiana
      State University Press, 1988.
112   Sedgwick, A., *The Ralliement in French Politics, 1890–98*, Harvard
      University Press, 1965.
113   O'Donnell, J. D., *Lavigerie in Tunisia, 1875–1892*, University of
      Georgia Press, 1979.
114   Lecomte, M., *Les Ralliés. Histoire d'un parti, 1886–1898*,
      Flammarion, 1898, p. 179.
115   Bonnefous, A., 'Les Royalistes du Nord et le Ralliement', *Revue du
      Nord*, xlvii, no. 184, pp. 29–48, 1965.
116   Sternhell, Z., 'National Socialism and Anti- Semitism: the case of
      Maurice Barrès, *Journal of Contemporary History*, vol. 8, no. 4,
      pp. 47–66, 1973.

117 Beau de Loménie, E., *Édouard Drumont ou l'Anticapitalisme national*, Pauvert, 1968.

118 Bouvier, J., *Les Deux Scandales de Panama*, 'Archives', Gallimard Julliard, 1964.

119 Sternhell, Z., *La Droite Révolutionnaire, 1885–1914. Les Origines françaises du Fascisme*, Seuil, 1978.

120 Wilson, S., *Ideology and Experience. Antisemitism in France at the Time of the Dreyfus Affair*, Fairleigh Dickinson University Press and Associated University Press, 1982.

121 Warshaw, D., *Paul Leroy-Beaulieu and Established Liberalism in France*, Northern Illinois University Press, 1991.

122 Prestwich, P. E., *Drink and the Politics of Social Reform: Antialcoholism in France since 1870*, Society for the Promotion of Science and Scholarship, 1988.

123 Elwitt, S., *The Third Republic Defended. Bourgeois Reform in France, 1880–1914*, Louisiana State University Press, 1986.

124 Mitchell, A., *The Divided Path. The German Influence on Social Reform in France after 1870*, University of North Carolina Press, 1991.

125 Scott, J. A., *Republican Ideas and the Liberal Tradition in France, 1870–1914*, Columbia University Press, 1951.

126 Haywood, J. E. S., 'The Official Social Philosophy of the Third Republic: Léon Bourgeois and Solidarism', *International Review of Social History*, 6, pp. 19–48, 1961.

127 Ruby, M., *Le Solidarisme*, Librairie Gedalge, 1971.

128 'Cent Ans de Catholicisme social dans la région du Nord. Actes du Colloque de Lille des 7 et 8 décembre 1990', *Revue du Nord*, pp. 290–1 avril–septembre, 1991.

129 Mayeur, J-M., *Une Prêtre démocrate: l'abbé Lemire, 1853–1928*, Casterman, Paris, 1968.

130 Ford, C., *Creating the Nation in Provincial France. Religion and Political Identity in Brittany*, Princeton University Press, 1993.

131 Mayeur, J-M., 'Les congrès nationaux de la Démocratie chrétienne à Lyon, 1896, 1897, 1898', *Revue d'histoire moderne et contemporaine* 9 (1962), reprinted in Mayeur, *Catholicisme social et démocratie chrétienne*, Armand Colin, 1986.

132 Rémond, R., *Les Deux Congrès ecclésiastiques de Reims et de Bourges, 1896–1900*, Sirey, Paris, 1964.

133 Burridge, W., *Destiny Africa. Cardinal Lavigerie and the Making of the White Fathers*, G. Chapman, 1966.

134 Brunschwig, H., *French Colonialism, 1871–1914. Myth and Reality*, Pall Mall Press, 1966.

135 Andrew C. M. and Kanya-Forstner, A. J., 'The French "colonial party": its composition, aims and influence, 1885– 1914', *Historical Journal*, xiv, pp. 99–128, 1971.

136   Bates, D., *The Fashoda Incident of 1898*, Oxford University Press, Oxford, 1984.
137   Levering Lewis, D., *The Race to Fashoda: European Colonisation and African Resistance in the Scramble for Africa*, Bloomsbury, 1988.

THE DREYFUS AFFAIR

138   Cahm, E., *The Dreyfus Affair in French Politics and Society*, Longman, 1996.
139   Kedward, H. R., *The Dreyfus Affair*, Longman, 1969.
140   Bredin, J-D., *The Affair. The Case of Alfred Dreyfus*, Sidgwick and Jackson, 1987.
141   Péguy, C., *Notre Jeunesse*, 1910, Gallimard, 1957.
142   Kleeblatt, N. L., ed., *The Dreyfus Affair, Art, Truth and Justice*, University of California Press, 1987. Chapter by Paula Hyman.
143   Burns, M., *Dreyfus. A Family Affair, 1789–1945*, Chatto and Windus, 1992.
144   Sorlin, P., *'La Croix' et les Juifs, 1880–1899. Contribution à l'histoire de l'antisémitisme contemporaine*, Grasset, Paris, 1967.
145   Winock, M., *Nationalisme, antisémitisme et fascisme*, Seuil, 1990.
146   Marrus, M., *The Politics of Assimilation. A Study of the French Jewish Community at the Time of the Dreyfus Affair*, Oxford University Press, Oxford, 1971.
147   Birnbaum, P., ed., *La France de l'Affaire Dreyfus*, Gallimard, 1994. Birnbaum argues against Marrus that Jews were closely involved in fighting anti-Semitism.
148   Delhorbe, C., *L'Affaire Dreyfus et les Écrivains français*, Neuchâtel-Paris, 1932.
149   Leroy, G., ed., *Les Écrivains et l'Affaire Dreyfus*, Presses Universitaires de France, 1983.
150   Ory P. and Sirinelle, J-F., *Les Intellectuels en France de l'Affaire Dreyfus à nos jours*, Armand Colin, 1986.
151   Zola, É., *La Vérité en Marche*, E. Fasquelle, 1901.
152   France, A., *L'Anneau d'Améthyste*, Calmann Lévy, 1899.
153   L'Amitié Charles Péguy, *Feuillets Mensuels*, 22, July 1951.
154   Smith, R. J., *The École Normale Supérieure and the Third Republic*, Albany, 1982.
155   Headings, M. J., *French Freemasonry under the Third Republic*, Johns Hopkins University Press, 1949.
156   Fitch, N., 'Mass Culture, Politics and Modern Anti-Semitism: the Dreyfus Affair in rural France', *American Historical Review*, 97/1, pp. 55–95, 1992.

157 Ponty, J., 'La Presse quotidienne et l'affaire Dreyfus en 1898–9', *Revue d'Histoire Moderne et Contemporaine*, 21, pp. 193–220, 1974.

158 Jaurès, J. and Guesde, J., *Les Deux Methodes*, 1900, 2nd edn Paris, 1925.

159 Glenn Brown, R., *Fashoda Reconsidered. The Impact of Domestic Politics on French Policy in Africa, 1893–98*, Johns Hopkins University Press, 1969.

160 Texier, R., *Le Fol Été de Fort Chabrol*, France-Empire, 1990.

161 Weber, E., *Action Française. Royalism and reaction in Twentieth-Century France*, Stanford University Press, 1962, reprinted 1969.

162 Porch, D., *The March to the Marne. The French Army, 1871–1914*, Cambridge University Press, Cambridge, 1981.

RADICALISM

163 Nordmann, J. T., *Histoire des Radicaux, 1820–1973*, La Table Ronde, 1974.

164 Nordmann, J. T., *La France Radicale*, 'Archives', Gallimard Julliard, 1977.

165 Berstein, S., *Histoire du Parti Radical*, I, Fondation Nationale des Sciences Politiques, 1980.

166 Baal, G., *Histoire du Radicalisme*, La Découverte, 1994.

167 Martin, B., 'The Creation of the Action Libérale Populaire', *French Historical Studies*, 9, pp. 660–89, 1976.

168 Sanson, R., 'Centre et Gauche (1901–1914): l'Alliance Républicaine Démocratique et le Parti Radical-Socialiste', *Revue d'Histoire Moderne et Contemporaine*, 39/3 pp. 493–512, juillet-septembre, 1992.

169 Guillemin, H., *L'Arrière Pensée de Jaurès*, Gallimard, 1966.

170 Berstein, S., 'La Politique sociale des Républicains' in Serge Berstein and Odile Rudelle eds, *Le Modèle républicain*, Presses Universitaires de France, 1992.

171 Stone, J. F., 'The Radicals and the Interventionist State: Attitudes, Ambiguities and Transformations, 1880–1914', French History 2/2 pp. 173–86, 1988.

172 Stone, J. F., *The Search for Social Peace: Reform Legislation in France, 1890–1914*, State University, New York. 1985.

173 Larkin, M., *Religion, Politics and Preferment in France since 1890. La Belle Époque and its Legacy*, Cambridge University Press, Cambridge, 1995.

174 Winnacker, R. A., 'The Délégation des Gauches', *Journal of Modern History*, 9, pp. 449–70, 1937.

175   Baal, G., 'Combes et la République des Comités', *Revue d'Histoire Moderne et Contemporaine*, 24, pp. 260–85, 1977.

176   Shorter E., and Tilly, C., *Strikes in France, 1830–1968*, Cambridge University Press, Cambridge, 1974.

177   Julliard, J., 'Jeune et vieux syndicat chez les mineurs du Pas-de-Calais', *Le Mouvement Social*, 47, pp. 7–30, 1964.

178   Wormser, C., *La République de Clemenceau*, Presses Universitaires de France, 1961.

179   Napo, F., *1907: La Révolte des Vignerons*, Privat, 1971.

180   Harvey Smith, J., 'Agricultural workers and the French winegrowers revolt of 1907', *Past and Present*, 79, 1978.

181   Julliard, J., *Clemenceau, briseur de grèves*, 'Archives', Gallimard Julliard, 1965.

182   Georges, B. and Tintant, D., *Léon Jouhaux, cinquante ans de syndicalisme, I. Des Origines à 1921*, Presses Universitaires de France, 1962.

183   Klejman, L. and Rochefort, F., *L'Égalité en Marche. Le Féminisme sous la Troisième République*, Fondation Nationale des Sciences Politiques, 1989.

184   Hause, S. and Kenney, A. R., *Women's Suffrage and Social Politics in the French Third Republic*, Princeton University Press, 1984.

185   Hause, S., *Hubertine Auclert. The French Suffragette*, Yale University Press, 1987.

186   Gordon, F., *The Integral Feminist: Madeleine Pelletier, 1874–1939*, University of Minnesota Press, 1990.

187   Sowerwine, C., *Sisters or Citizens? Women and Socialism in France since 1876*, Cambridge University Press, Cambridge, 1982.

188   Young, R. J., *Power and Pleasure. Louis Barthou and the Third Republic*, McGill-Queens University Press, 1991.

189   Bredin, J-D., *Joseph Caillaux*, Hachette, 1980.

190   Berenson, E., *The Trial of Madame Caillaux*, University of California Press, 1992.

NATIONALISM

191   Digeon, C., *La Crise Allemande de la Pensée française, 1870–1914*, Presses Universitaires de France, 1959, new edn, PUF, 1992.

192   Général Trochu, *L'Armée Française en 1867*, 18, Amyot, Paris, 1867.

193   Gambetta, L., speech of 26 June 1871, in *Discours*, vol. ii, Paris, 1881.

194   Roberts, J. M., 'The Paris Commune from the Right', *English Historical Review*, 1973.

195   Krumeich, G., 'Joan of Arc between right and left' in Robert Tombs ed., *Nationalism and nationhood in France. From Boulangism to the Great War, 1889–1918*, pp. 63–73, HarperCollins Academic, 1991.

196 Harris, R., *Lourdes: Body and Spirit in the Secular Age*, forthcoming.
197 Marx, K., *The Civil War in France*, International Working Men's Association, 1921.
198 Gildea, R., *The Past in French History*, p. 139, Yale University Press, 1994.
199 Nora, P., 'Ernest Lavisse. Son rôle dans la formation du sentiment national', *Revue Historique* 228, pp. 73–106, 1962. Republished as 'Lavisse, instituteur national' in Pierre Nora ed., *Les Lieux de Mémoire*, I, pp. 274–89, Gallimard, 1984.
200 Baumgart, W., *Imperialism. The Idea and Reality of British and French Colonial Expansion, 1880–1914*, Oxford University Press, Oxford, 1982.
201 Bédarida, F., 'L'Armée et la République. Les opinions politiques des officiers français', *Revue Historique*, 232, pp. 119–164, 1964.
202 Rémond, R., *L'Anticlericalisme en France de 1815 à nos jours*, Fayard, Paris, 1976.
203 Challener, R. D., *The French Theory of the Nation in Arms, 1866–1939*, New York, Columbia, 1955, pp. 39–40.
204 Mitchell, A., '"A Situation of Inferiority". French military reorganization after the defeat of 1870', *American Historical Review*, 86/1, pp. 49–62, 1981.
205 Pedroncini, G., ed., *Histoire militaire de la France III. De 1870 à 1940*, PUF, 1992.
206 Jauffret, J-C., 'Armée et pouvoir politique. La question des troupes spéciales chargés du maintien de l'ordre en France de 1871 à 1914', *Revue Historique*, 270, pp. 98–144, 1983.
207 Rabaut, J., *L'Antimilitarisme en France, 1870–1975*, Hachette, 1975.
208 Schneider, W. H., *An Empire for the Masses. The French Popular Image of Africa, 1870–1900*, Greenwood Press, 1982.
209 Baubérot, J., 'L'Antiprotestantisme politique à la fin du XIXe siècle', *Revue d'Histoire et de Philosophie des Religions*, 52, pp. 449–84, 1972; 53, pp. 177–221, 1973.
210 Sternhell, Z., *Maurice Barrès et le Nationalisme français*, Armand Colin, 1972.
211 Girardet, R., *Le Nationalisme français, 1871–1914*, Armand Colin, 1966.
212 Weber, E., *The Nationalist Revival in France, 1905–1914*, University of California Press, 1959.
213 Silverman, D. P., *Reluctant Union. Alsace-Lorraine and Imperial Germany, 1871–1918*, Pennsylvania State University, 1972.
214 Keiger, J. F., *France and the Origins of the First World War*, Macmillan, 1983.
215 Wright, G., *Poincaré and the French Presidency*, Stanford University Press, 1942.
216 Julliard, J., 'La C.G.T. devant la guerre, 1900–1914', *Le Mouvement Social*, 49, pp. 47–62, 1964.

217   Fiechter, J-J., *Le Socialisme français de l'Affaire Dreyfus à la Grande Guerre*, Droz, 1965.
218   Haupt, G., *Socialism and the Great War*, Oxford University Press, 1972.
219   Milner, S., *The Dilemmas of Internationalism. French Syndicalism and the International Labour Movement, 1900–1914*, Berg, 1990.
220   Becker, J-J., *The Great War and the French People*, Berg, 1985.

THE THIRD REPUBLIC ASSESSED

221   Lévy-Leboyer, M. and Bourguignon, F., *The French Economy in the Nineteenth Century*, CUP/Maison des Sciences de l'Homme, 1990.
222   Wylie, L., *Village in the Vaucluse*, Harvard University Press, 1957.
223   Crouzet, F., ed., *The Economic Development of France since 1870*, Edward Elgar Publishing Co., 1993.
224   Caron, F., *An Economic History of Modern France*, Methuen, 1979.
225   Ferro, M., *The Great War, 1914–1918*, Routledge and Kegan Paul, 1973.

INDEX

Action Française, 57, 77
Agriculture, 24–5, 42, 81
Algeria, 54, 109
Allemane, Jean, 35. 40
Alsace-Lorraine, 73, 78, 85, 107
anarchism, 34, 40–1, 55, 64, 96–7, 105–6
anarcho-syndicalism, 41, 64, 65–6, 97
anticlericalism, 8, 15, 17, 19, 26, 44, 49, 63–5, 78, 92–3, 103
antimilitarism, 74, 77, 78, 111
anti-Semitism, 44–5, 51–2, 54, 55, 57
army, 2, 4, 20, 38, 51, 65, 66, - 73–5, 101–2
Auclert, Hubertine, 69
Austria-Hungary, 73, 111

Barrès, Maurice, 44, 57, 76, 78, 82
Barthou, Louis, 61, 65, 69–70, 79
Bismarck, Otto von, 4, 18, 20, 73, 109
Basly, Émile, 65, 66, 93
Blanqui, Auguste, 4, 37
Blanquists, 4, 21, 22, 23, 36, 64
Bloc des Gauches, 63–4, 74
Blum, Léon, 54, 100–1
Bonapartism, 3, 6, 7, 8, 10, 16, 19, 21, 77
Boulanger, General Georges, 12, 19–20, 21–3, 37, 74, 94
Boulangism, 13, 17, 21, 37, 44, 94–5
Bourgeois, Léon, 11, 46–7, 60
Bourgeoisie, 30–1

Bourses du Travail, 28, 30, 35–6, 38, 64, 66
Briand, Aristide, 36, 65, 67–8, 69, 84
Brisson, Henri, 55, 56, 58, 60
Broglie, Duc de, 7, 8
Brousse, Paul, 34, 35
Buisson, Ferdinand, 68

Caillaux, Henriette, 70, 79
Caillaux, Joseph, 61, 62, 65, 67, 69–70, 78, 79, 84
Carmaux, 38, 40
Carnot, Sadi, 10, 21, 40
Casimir-Périer, Auguste, 7
Casimir-Périer, Jean, 106
Cassagnac, Paul de, 19
Catholic Church, 8, 15, 17–18, 48–9, 59, 63, 71, 78
Cavaignac, Godfrey, 55–6
Chamber of Deputies, 7, 8, 10, 12–14, 39, 90–2
Chambord, Comte de, 5, 9, 87
Cheysson, Émile, 46
Christian Democracy, 48
Clemenceau, Georges, 17, 18, 20, 22, 45, 53, 55, 60, 65, 66, 67, 68–9, 73, 74, 77, 82, 83, 105–6, 109
colonies, 18–19, 49–50, 109
Combes, Émile, 63–4, 65
Commune, Paris, 1–2, 4–5, 6, 17, 34, 36, 46, 72, 87
Confédération Générale du Travail (CGT), 28, 30, 36, 64, 65–6, 77, 79
Constans, Ernest, 23

Constitution of 1875: 7–8, 18, 81–2
Corruption, Political 14, 82, 90–1

Daudet, Alphonse, 73
defeat of 1871: 1, 71–3
Delcassé, Théophile, 11, 56, 82
Delesalle, Paul, 41
Democratic Alliance, 61, 63, 67, 69
Déroulède, Paul, 18, 20, 22, 23, 57, 59, 60, 72, 73, 76
Dillon, Count, 21, 73
Dreyfus Affair, 51–9, 60, 75, 100–3
Drumont, Édouard, 44–5, 52, 54
Dupuy, Charles, 45, 56

education, 17, 29, 30–1
Egypt, 19, 50
elections, legislative
    (1869), 2
    (1871), 3
    (1876), 8
    (1877), 8
    (1881), 10
    (1885), 19
    (1889), 23, 42
    (1893), 38, 45, 50
    (1898), 54, 55, 61
    (1902), 63
    (1906), 65
    (1910), 67–8
    (1914), 69
Esterhazy, Major, 53, 101, 102
Étienne, Eugène, 50
Eudes, Émile, 36, 61

Falloux, Comte de, 5, 9
Fashoda, 56, 102–3
Faure, Félix, 49, 57
Faure, Sébastien, 40, 41
Ferroul, Ernest, 39, 93
Ferry, Jules, 10, 12, 17, 18, 20–1, 56, 73, 82, 83, 93, 94–5, 109
Floquet, Charles, 19, 21, 22, 23, 45, 60
Fourmies, 38, 40

France, Anatole, 53–4, 100
Franco-Russian alliance, 10, 49
Freemasonry, 54, 64, 76
French Section of the Workers' International (SFIO), 64, 66, 69, 70, 78, 79
French Union for Women's Suffrage, 69
Freycinet, Charles de, 8, 10, 11, 20, 21, 45, 109

Gallifet, General Gaston, 58
Gambetta, Léon, 1–2, 5–6, 8, 9, 10, 12, 13, 17, 71, 72, 73, 86, 89–90, 92
general strike, 36, 41, 77, 97
Germany, 18, 20, 69, 72, 73, 77, 79, 80, 81, 85, 110
Goblet, René, 19, 20, 60
Government of National Defence, 2–3, 72, 107
Granger, Ernest, 36, 37
Grave, Jean, 34, 40, 41
Great Britain, 50, 56–7, 77, 85
Grévy, Jules, 9, 10, 19, 20, 21
Griffuelhes, Victor, 64, 66
Guérin, Jules, 54, 57, 59
Guesde, Jules, 34, 35, 36, 37, 55, 61–2, 64, 79, 96
Guesdists, 37, 38–9, 65

Hansi, 78
Harmel, Léon, 48
Henry, Colonel, 56
Henry, Émile, 40, 96–7
Herr, Lucien, 54
Hervé, Gustave, 77
Hugo, Victor, 72, 76

Immigration, 27
Indo-China, 18, 19, 73, 74, 109
Industry, 26–7, 31, 32
Intellectuals, 53–4, 57, 101–2
International, Workers', 4, 33, 38, 41, 64, 85
Italy, 73, 110

Jacobinism, 4, 12, 58, 83
Jaurès, Jean, 38, 55, 60, 61–2, 64, 70, 78, 105, 106, 111–12
Jérôme-Napoléon, Prince, 19, 21
Jews, 51–2, 54, 75
Joan of Arc, 59, 71, 78, 79, 85
Jouhaux, Léon, 66, 111

Lafargue, Paul, 34, 37, 38
Laguerre, Georges, 22, 23
Lamy, Étienne, 43, 45
Lavigerie, Cardinal, 44, 49
Lavisse, Ernest, 72
Lazare, Bernard, 52
League of Rights of Man, 54
Legitimism, 5, 6, 7, 8, 16, 19
Lemire, Abbé Jules, 48
Leo XIII, Pope, 44, 48
Leroy-Beaulieu, Paul, 45–6
Liberal Action Party, 61
Ligue de la Patrie Française, 57, 76
Ligue des Patriotes, 18, 20, 22, 23, 73, 76
Loubet, Émile, 12, 57, 58
Loynes, Madame de, 31
Lumière Brothers, 31

Mackau, Baron de, 19. 20, 21
MacMahon, Marshal, 6, 7, 8
Madagascar, 30, 74
Malon, Benoît, 37
Marchand, Captain J.-B., 50, 56, 102–3
Marx, Karl, 33, 34, 52
Marxism, 34, 39, 41
Maupassant, Guy de, 82
Maurras, Charles, 77, 78, 79, 84, 110
Méline, Jules, 11, 43, 46, 47, 49, 55, 61, 75, 83, 99–100
Mercier, General, 53, 58
Michel, Louise, 41
Millerand, Alexandre, 38, 39, 55, 58, 60, 61, 62, 64, 84, 104–5
Morocco crises:
(1905), 77

(1911), 61, 78–9
Motte, Eugène, 61
Mun, Albert de, 5, 19, 21, 44, 48, 61, 64, 69, 79, 93

Napoleon III, 2, 10, 21
National Assembly (1871–5), 2–3, 5
National Guard, 4, 74
nationalism, 51, 56–7, 67, 71–3, 75–9, 84–5, 107–8, 111–12
Neuville, Alphonse de, 72
nobility, 31–2

Opportunism, 11, 16, 17–21, 22, 43, 44
Orleanism, 3, 7, 8, 12, 16, 19, 20
Orléans, Duc d', 57

Panama Scandal, 45, 52, 55, 60
Paris, 3, 4, 15, 29, 30, 35, 36, 37, 38, 40, 54, 61, 63, 65, 72
Paris, Comte de, 5, 6, 19, 21
peasantry, 23–6, 80, 83
Péguy, Charles, 51–2, 54, 55, 59, 79
Pelletan, Camille, 62, 103–4
Pelletier, Madeleine, 69
Pelloutier, Fernand, 36, 41, 97
petite bourgeoisie, the, 28–30
Picquart, Lieut.-Col., 52
Piou, Jacques, 43, 45, 61, 98
Poincaré, Raymond, 12, 61, 69, 79, 82
Popular Liberal Action, 64
Possibilism, 35, 37, 40
Pouget, Émile, 40, 41, 64
Presidency of the Republic, the, 6, 7, 8, 10, 18, 82
Press, The, 14, 54–5
Progressists, 47, 61
Protestantism, 50, 56, 71, 75–6
Proudhon, Pierre-Joseph, 33
Proust, Marcel, 53
Prussia, 1, 3, 4, 71, 72

radicalism, 7, 13, 16, 17–21, 22, 23, 47
Radical party, 60–1, 62–4, 66–70, 79, 103–4
railways, 18, 62, 67, 83
Ralliement, the, 43–4, 98–100
Raoul-Duval, Edgar, 20
Ravachol, 40
Reinach, Jacques de, 45
Reinach, Joseph, 52
Renan, Ernest, 72–3, 77, 107–8, 110
Renault Brothers, 31
Republican Federation, 61, 67
republican concentration, 16, 19, 45
republican defence, 58, 63
republican legitimacy, 9, 11, 16, 23, 83
Rochefort, Henri, 22, 23, 60
Rouvier, Maurice, 11, 20, 45, 61, 64, 67, 83
royalism, 2, 3, 5, 6–7, 12, 19, 21, 23, 43, 44, 51, 57, 77, 87–8, 98, 110
Russia, 49, 65, 79

Scheurer-Kestner, Auguste, 56
Schneider, Eugène, 32
Second Empire, 1, 2, 3, 10, 13, 17
Sedan, 2, 73
Senate, 7–8, 9, 10, 11–12, 18, 23, 47, 56
separation of Church and State, 65, 78, 85
Siegfried, Jules, 46

Simon, Jules, 8, 86, 93
Singer, Winaretta, 32
socialism, 4, 22, 33–41, 55, 58, 61–2, 64–5, 96
Social Reform, 46–8, 62–3, 64, 67, 79, 104–5
Solidarism, 47

tariffs, 18, 25, 42–3
Thiers, Adolphe, 2, 3, 4, 5, 6, 8, 10, 72, 74, 88–9
trade unions, 27–8, 35, 65–6, 67, 69, 107
Trochu, General, 71
Tunisia, 18, 49, 73, 109

Union Sacrée, the, 79, 85
universal suffrage, 2, 3, 6, 7, 10, 12–13, 37, 39, 60, 68, 86
Uzès, Duchesse d', 21

Vaillant, Auguste, 40
Vaillant, Édouard, 36, 37, 58
Versailles, 4, 85
Viviani, René, 65, 68, 79

Waldeck-Rousseau, René, 46, 58, 61, 62, 63, 64, 82
Wilson, Daniel, 20, 21
women, 16, 27, 30, 68–9, 83
working classes, 26–8, 30, 34, 36, 38–9, 65–6

Zola, Émile, 35, 40, 53, 54, 59, 77, 101–2